# A NEW LOOK AT
# NEEDLEPOINT

The Wedding Pillow is worked on 14 count mono canvas in Persian yarns and metal thread. The Tree of Life is worked in Tent stitch, and the surrounding sky is in Brick. Stem with Backstitching makes up the grass. The cat and bride's dress and veil are worked in Split Gobelin, the groom's coat is Gobelin Droit. The yellow sky of "The Other World" is worked in Diagonal Tent, the tree is Oblong with Backstitch and Ribbed Spiders. The female creature is in Diagonal Mosaic and her mate in Byzantine. The grass is an uneven count Gobelin Droit. Metal thread French Knots decorate the creatures' antlers and the bride's costume. Silver Backstitching and Couching decorate the groom's coat. Designed and worked by Carol Rome, inspired by a fabric painting by Nancy Carroll. Courtesy of Mr. and Mrs. D. Malcolm Leith, Washington, D.C.

# A NEW LOOK AT

# NEEDLEPOINT

## The Complete Guide to Canvas Embroidery

by **CAROL CHENEY ROME**
and **GEORGIA FRENCH DEVLIN**

Crown Publishers, Inc., New York

TO

Dick and Bob

Photography by William B. Hubbell, Jr., and Carol Cheney Rome
Stitch diagrams by Dunham & Hunter, Inc.
Drawings by Carol Cheney Rome

© 1972 by Carol Cheney Rome and Georgia French Devlin

ISBN: 0-517-500167
ISBN: 0-517-511185

Designed by Ruth Smerechniak

Printed in the United States of America

Published simultaneously in Canada by General Publishing Company Limited

Third Printing, July, 1973

# Acknowledgments

We owe credit for the production of this book to many people. Special thanks are due to Mrs. W. A. Camp, without whose expert assistance the chapters on projects and finishing could not have been written; and to Stephen Walsh, whose tireless efforts are responsible for the stitch diagrams. Our deep appreciation is due to Christian Inkley Manuel, who gave many hours of help in editing and proofreading the manuscript.

Thanks also to Bruce Shelby and Wayne Lieber who developed and printed many of the photographs in the book and to Eric Glueck and Tim Waite who supplemented the photography by Mrs. Rome and Mr. Hubbell. Mrs. George French, Jr., Louise C. French, and Page Wells are to be thanked for acting as project scouts.

We are grateful to the museums which provided illustrations of heritage canvas embroidery and advice on the history of needlepoint and to the chapters of the Embroiderers' Guild of America and the many individuals who so generously contributed photographs of their finished work to illustrate this manuscript. The experience of writing this book has been greatly enriched by our communications with canvas embroiderers all over the country.

Last but not least, we acknowledge the encouragement of our editor, Brandt Aymar, and we thank our husbands, family, and friends for their patience, advice, and understanding of the priority this project had on our time.

C.C.R. and G.F.D.

# List of Color Plates

# Contents

# CHAPTER 1

# Introduction
# to Needlepoint

Section of a headboard worked in decorative needlepoint stitches by Mrs. H. Weller
Keever, New Canaan, Connecticut. Designed by Dorothy Kaestner.

Modern version of the American flag by Louise C. French, Milwaukee.

Louis XVI style love seat worked in Diagonal Tent by Mrs. H. P. Wilson, Jr., Denver.

# THE PLEASURES OF NEEDLEPOINT AS A HOBBY

The self-conscious days when store-bought articles were glorified and home-made articles were despised are finally over. There is a reverse trend taking place in which people once again have learned to admire the beauty and originality of handcrafted articles to wear, adorn the home or give as gifts. People are constantly seeking ways to counteract the impersonality of life in the age of technology; they are more and more attracted to activities in which they create something from start to finish.

One of the nicest features of taking up needlepoint as a hobby is that you need very little equipment to get started. Some canvas and yarn, a needle and a pair of scissors will set you up for your first project. Also, needlepoint is an activity that can be interrupted frequently without ill effects, making it ideal to take on errands where you will probably have to wait or on trips when you will have extra time on airplanes or in the car.

Beginners can achieve excellent results with their first attempts at needlepoint, which is not necessarily true of many other artistic endeavors. This is one reason why needlepoint makes a very good project for children.

It is not surprising that needlepoint has been used successfully in rehabilitative therapy because the actual process of stitching is relaxing and satisfying. The satisfaction of the work can be doubled when the design is your own. The finished work is very durable, and you may come to think of each piece in process as a potential heirloom.

A revival of the quilting bee idea has come about through creative embroidery. Many groups of interested stitchers have been formed to share ideas and questions, run workshops and enjoy their hobby together. Projects for church and synagogue or charity causes have resulted in rugs, wall hangings and other lovely articles made by a group effort and an inspiration for all to view.

The information in this book has been organized to provide you with all

Pooh Bear wall hanging by Mrs. William L. Scott, Denver. Pooh is worked in Diagonal Tent; the background is an "invented" stitch combining Tent with a buttonhole stitch.

Leopard in flowers. A canvas embroidery picture by Marina Spheeris, Milwaukee. Designed by Subo.

the basics for working projects from the simplest to the most complex. An attempt has been made to cover topics often not treated in other sources. You will learn the history of needlepoint. You will learn how to choose and work with the raw materials that go into canvas embroidery and how to care for your supplies. You will learn many stitches that are used in needlepoint and how to design your own work. In addition, you will learn how to finish and mount your own projects with a minimum of expense and bother.

It is hoped that you will gain a great deal of pride and pleasure from the needlepoint pieces you create as a result of your new-found knowledge. It should give you a feeling of satisfaction to know that you are carrying on a tradition of decorative art that has existed for centuries and which has produced exquisite handcrafted articles.

## A BRIEF HISTORY OF CANVAS EMBROIDERY

The origins and development of embroidery are fraught with confusion, conflicting stories and missing links. The perishability of embroidered articles has left historians very few examples with which to document their research, and often they have had to turn to secondary sources such as sculptures and paintings for knowledge of their subject.

One historian theorizes that embroidery has been looked down on as feminine, a possible reason for its lack of popularity as a subject for research. It is true that many of the decorative arts are just beginning to receive the study they deserve. This is probably due to the public's renewed interest in all forms of handicrafts—a rebellion against mass production.

In presenting the subject of needlepoint historically, the first confusion that must be dealt with is the name! Even in many recent editions of dictionaries, needlepoint is defined as a kind of lace pattern worked with a needle instead of bobbins. At the same time, the word has come into popular usage as meaning embroidery worked with a needle over the counted threads of a canvas—a synonym for canvas embroidery.

It is possible that the second meaning of needlepoint comes from "needle painting," a term that reflects the high degree of artistry first associated with the ecclesiastical embroideries of the Middle Ages and more recently associated with the process of creating canvas embroidery. Whatever the true story, the terms "canvas embroidery" and "needlepoint" are now used interchangeably.

There are two factors that distinguish canvas embroidery from other kinds of embroidery. First, the stitches are worked over counted threads in prescribed patterns that follow the "grid" of the canvas; and second, the embroidery entirely covers the grounding canvas to form a new fabric.

Crewel embroidery, which is very popular today, is usually worked on linen or cotton fabric with wool yarn in pastoral or floral motifs. The stitchery does not cover the entire grounding fabric, and the stitches do not conform to the weave of the fabric, but are more random and free-flowing than canvas embroidery stitches.

It is very difficult to make a clear distinction between canvas embroidery and other kinds of embroidery when analyzing origins and development. It appears that most kinds of embroidery have one prototypical ancestor from which the various styles and techniques have evolved as the work became specialized in the hands of artisans and as new improvements were made in the manufacture of raw materials and tools.

The primitive forerunner of embroidery is the simple lacing stitch which led to basket-weaving and subsequently to embroidery. Examples of embroidered garments have been found in Egyptian tombs, and it is thought that the sails of the Nile River boats were embroidered for ceremonial purposes and commercial identification. The peoples of Asia Minor are known to have used needles to embellish fabric with embroidery, and embroidered robes were thought precious enough by the ancient Greeks to offer as gifts to their gods. Embroidery was also developing in other parts of the world. This craft was considered equal to painting in early Chinese and Japanese history.

Later, closer to the time of Christ, the Romans developed a kind of work that may have been similar to Tent and Cross stitch. This work was called *opus pulvinarium*, and it was used to strengthen fabric for garments.

Not much is known about the development of European and English embroidery until the thirteen and fourteenth centuries A.D., when a type of embroidery called *opus anglicanum* developed in England. Although this work is documented by ancient deeds and inventories, there is no record of the exact stitches used.

*Opus anglicanum* was ecclesiastical; many biblical scenes and stories of favorite saints were depicted in a rich array of threads, gems and beads. The backgrounds of these embroideries were almost exclusively sewn with gold-covered thread couched down with silk. The finished pieces, which sometimes were given as gifts of state or church, were highly valued all over Europe. The work was done in convents, monasteries and in the royal houses by both men and women. It somewhat resembled pages of the exquisite illuminated manuscripts of the day.

Ecclesiastical embroidery continued to be the major work done until the introduction of heraldry. Then a class of embroidery that was more secular than religious came into its own. It is thought that the custom of embroidering heraldic insignia on banners, horse gear, garments and household items was started as a means of recognition and to prevent confusion on the battlefield. Later, the use of these emblems became a birthright and a matter of family pride.

Interest in ecclesiastical embroidery began to wane as military and heraldic subjects became more popular. Also, ecclesiastical embroidery may have declined further as a result of the closing down of many convents and monasteries during the reign of Henry VIII. His patronage of embroidery, as

Bag (forel) embroidered in silk and metal thread, 14th-century French. *Courtesy of The Metropolitan Museum of Art, The Cloisters Collection, 1946.*

Cushion embroidered on canvas in silks and metal threads, first half of the 17th century, English. Note the raised work. *Courtesy of The Metropolitan Museum of Art, Rogers Fund, 1929.*

Fragment probably of a table cover worked in Cross stitch and Florentine stitch in pink, yellow, and green silk thread, 16th-century Spanish. *Courtesy of the Cooper-Hewitt Museum of Design, Smithsonian Institution, New York.*

8

Orpheus charming the beasts with music. Silk and metal threads on canvas, early 17th-century English. *Courtesy of The Metropolitan Museum of Art, Rogers Fund, 1910.*

Small panel of linen, solidly worked in silks and metal threads depicting various plants and creatures, 17th-century English. *Courtesy of the Cooper-Hewitt Museum of Design, Smithsonian Institution, New York.*

Needlepoint fire screen panel worked in wools on linen canvas around 1730, England. The design of flowers in a vase was a very popular theme. *Courtesy of the Colonial Williamsburg Foundation.*

Seat for a George I chair worked in wools and silk on linen canvas in Tent and Cross stitch, English 1725–35. The scene shows two ladies in elegant contemporary dress. *Courtesy of the Colonial Williamsburg Foundation.*

An unfinished chair seat cover worked in wools and silk on linen canvas about 1730, England. The variation of threads and stitches adds texture and luster to the piece. *Courtesy of the Colonial Williamsburg Foundation.*

well as Mary Queen of Scots', helped to popularize the craft, and people began to concentrate on adorning their homes and personal costumes.

This royal patronage was to be continued by Elizabeth I in the late sixteenth and early seventeenth centuries, at which time embroidery, including needlepoint, flourished. Steel needles were introduced in this era, which made the work easier and faster than with the previously used bone needles.

Embroidery became such an important industry in England that a guild was formed by artisans to regulate the quality of embroidered goods, among other things. Even before it was formally chartered in 1561, the Broderer's Company was very active and at one point was successful in getting Parliament to curb abuses in connection with imported Italian goldwork.

It is thought that the increased interest in tapestry in the sixteenth and seventeenth centuries concurrently led to an increased production of embroidery made to imitate tapestry. This has led to the confusion of canvas embroidery with tapestry, which actually is a decorative woven fabric created on a loom.

Pattern books became available and engravings were circulated for design ideas. Almost all young ladies received instruction in various forms of needlework.

By the nineteenth century, needlepoint canvas was being machine-made. In addition, the aniline dyes were developed, giving rise to a whole new range of bright, garish yarn colors. Victorian ladies began to rely less on their own ingenuity and talents and fell prey to fads. They went wild over the aniline-dyed yarns and a type of mechanically produced charted designs,

Berlin work chair cover, late 19th-century English or American. The colors are purple, pink, red, green, and black—all aniline dyed wool yarn. *Courtesy of the Cooper-Hewitt Museum of Design, Smithsonian Institution, New York.*

now referred to as Berlin work. This work is characterized by its harsh colors and stereotyped floral designs. Often black was used for the background, and the Tent stitch was used almost exclusively. This canvas embroidery comes as a real disappointment to the modern viewer after the beautifully crafted, home-inspired work of earlier days.

Canvas embroidery did not flourish in the colonial days of America. Materials were scarce, and the women were occupied with stitching essentials and had little time for fancy work. One scholar speculates that the subjects of the embroideries of the Stuart reigns were too "royalist" for the Puritan women.

What embroidery was done in the very early days of America was in the form of samplers containing alphabets and pious sayings worked by young fingers. These samplers followed in the tradition of those which had been carefully stitched since before the time of printing. They were originally used as a record of ornamental lettering and numerals for marking household linens. Embroidery caught on in America in the nineteenth century and since then has shown a fairly steady increase in popularity.

Tent stitch has been used in canvas work since the earliest days. Many people have the mistaken idea that needlepoint is represented only by this stitch. However, this form of embroidery may embrace over two hundred stitches, all of which form a different textured pattern when worked over canvas. Turkey Tufting was extremely popular in Elizabethan England. The Gobelin stitches were developed to imitate tapestry. Examples of many stitches such as Smyrna, Crossed Corners and Rococo can be found in samplers and other heritage pieces.

People have been influenced by social and religious themes in their choice of designs, and scenes of nature have been used extensively since the beginning of canvas embroidery. The flower is probably the single most popular motif, and has been carried over for centuries, its rendering on canvas reflecting the styles and modes of the day.

Canvas embroidery has a venerable history. Fine threads and gems have gone into its making as well as untold hours of fastidious work by men and women alike. It has been sought after by kings and has adorned the robes of bishops and the altars of the most famous cathedrals. Canvas embroidery has found a place in the domestic scene to brighten dark rooms and embellish the trousseaus of young maidens. Children have learned their letters and numbers by stitching samplers, and young women have stitched wallets for their loved ones.

Some of the work has not been beautiful, and some of it has been ill designed and poorly executed. However, it all represents a decorative art that has withstood the passing vogues of centuries to enjoy a renaissance in our day that is giving rise to thousands of lovely pieces as well as thousands of hours of pleasure and creativity to those who do the work.

Sarah Bradstreet's sampler, dated 1752. The verse in this New England girl's sampler reads, "Adam and Eve whilst innocent, in paradise were plac'd, but soon the serpent by his wiles, the happy pair disgrac'd." *Courtesy of the Historic Deerfield Collection, Deerfield, Massachusetts.*

The "Reclining Shepherdess" scene was stitched in Boston in the mid-18th century. Note the black sheep near the man's foot. *Courtesy of the Historic Deerfield Collection, Deerfield, Massachusetts.*

This chair seat is worked on very fine gauge canvas. The design is arranged so that there is practically no background. French knots are used in the centers of some of the flowers. 18th-century American. *Courtesy of the Historic Deerfield Collection, Deerfield, Massachusetts.*

These chair seat covers were worked in the early 18th century, probably in America. Tent and Cross stitches are used to work the designs, which seem primitive compared with some of the earlier European and English work. *Courtesy of Bayou Bend Collection, The Museum of Fine Arts, Houston.*

# CHAPTER 2

# Getting Started

## INTRODUCTION

This chapter describes the raw materials that go into a needlepoint project as well as how to care for and handle them. The quality of the finished pieces you turn out is dependent on the quality of the supplies you use. Don't "chinch" when purchasing canvas and yarns. Many hours of thought and work will go into making up the project, and it is not worth the few pennies you might save to work with inferior products. Being an alert consumer may save you from the discouraging experience of spending weeks on a piece only to have the colors bleed or the canvas threads break beyond repair.

Since you are investing in fine raw materials, you won't want to cut corners in caring for them. There are many practical hints in this chapter aimed at helping you get the maximum benefits out of your initial investment. In addition, this chapter should provide you with most of the necessary basics of canvas embroidery to get you started on an enthusiastic binge of stitching!

## CANVAS

There are two kinds of needlepoint canvas both commonly made of cotton. Good needlepoint canvas is heavily sized to keep the threads in place. Avoid buying canvas that has obvious flaws, such as knots, thin or frayed places, or nubs. Be sure it is squarely woven and that it is stiff, shiny and crisp. You can work on either surface of the canvas—there is no right or wrong side.

*Mono,* or "uni" canvas, is woven with single vertical and horizontal threads intersecting. It is available in white, yellow, or tan. Mono is the general, all-purpose canvas. It is easy on the eyes because the spaces between the canvas threads are relatively large and well defined. In addition, there is no confusion in calculating stitch counts over the single intersections of mono canvas.

*Penelope* canvas probably is named after Ulysses' wife, a famous legendary needlewoman. In Ulysses' long absence, Penelope thwarted the advances of suitors by asking them to wait until she finished weaving a garment, secretly undoing the day's work every night to delay its completion.

Penelope canvas is made up of pairs of vertical and horizontal threads, and it comes in white or tan. The pairs of threads in Penelope can be picked apart to form an area of "half-size" mono canvas. This allows you the option of working some of the design twice as small as the rest on the same piece of canvas. This feature is particularly useful when working sections of fine detail.

Both mono and Penelope canvas are available in several sizes or gauges. The size refers to the number of canvas threads per inch, and hence the number of stitches that can be worked per inch. There are three main size categories: petit point, which is fine gauge canvas (16 or more mesh per inch); gros point, which is medium gauge canvas (8 to 15 mesh per inch); and quick point, large gauge rug canvas (3 to 7 mesh per inch).

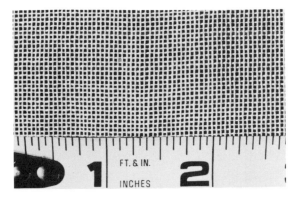

24 count mono canvas

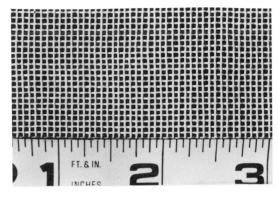

18 count mono canvas

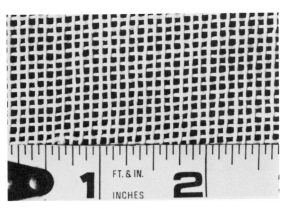

12 count mono canvas

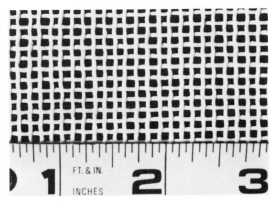

10 count mono canvas

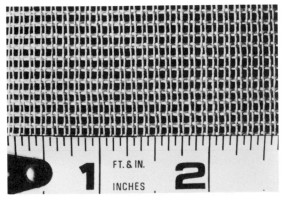

10 count Penelope canvas

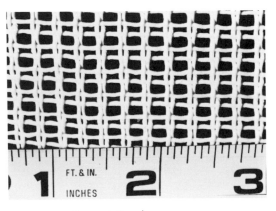

5 count Penelope canvas

4 count rug canvas

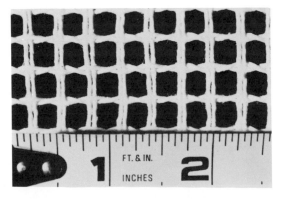

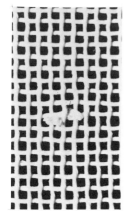

The knotted thread in this canvas may pull apart during a work session or in the blocking process. Avoid buying flawed canvas.

These canvases are sold in different widths. Generally, the fine canvas is made narrower than the large gauge canvas. The range is from 24″ to 60″, with most gauges available in 36″ to 40″ widths.

The color of canvas you choose is strictly a matter of personal preference and will have no significant effect on the end result. The nonwhite canvases have slightly less glare.

Choose the canvas according to the specifics of the projects you are planning, keeping in mind the following considerations. Fine gauge canvas allows for detail and a finished piece that is lightweight. It is relatively hard on the eyes and is slow to work up. Large gauge canvas makes up into bulky finished pieces, is suitable for large, simple designs, is easy on the eyes and works up quickly.

For most projects, you will find the middle range canvas, around 13 or 14 count, the easiest to work with and the best all-purpose size.

Before cutting the canvas, measure the dimensions of your project carefully and add any extra area that will be needed in the finishing process. In other words, you will needlepoint the size of the design *plus* any extra needed to make the finished piece "fit" when it is made up. These specifications can be found in Chapter 5: Projects. If you are planning to make a border, add the extra inches to the design dimensions.

In addition to these dimensions, you should always add an extra 1½″ to 2″ margin on all sides of the design. This will be left unstitched and will be used during the blocking process after the piece is needlepointed.

Blank canvas should be left on each side of the design. Mini-sampler by Page Wells, Houston.

Do not cut the canvas to conform to the exact "ins and outs" of the design, even though there may be curves and rounded areas. Leave the canvas square or rectangular or you will not be able to block the finished piece back to its original shape. Trim any excess canvas off *after* the project is blocked.

The cut edges of canvas fray and ravel very easily and should be bound in some way immediately after cutting. The edges can be taped with masking or freezer tape. This is an easy, inexpensive and generally effective method of protecting the edges. In some cases, when the finished piece will have to be subjected to rigorous wet blocking, it is better to secure the edges with seam tape sewn by hand or by machine. You can also use iron-on seam binding.

From here on, canvas threads are referred to as "mesh" to distinguish them easily from yarn strands and threads.

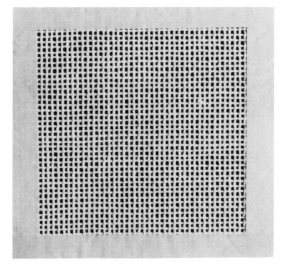

Taping the cut canvas edges will prevent raveling.

The cut canvas edges can be hemmed instead of taped to prevent raveling.

Rug yarn, Persian yarn, tapestry yarn, and embroidery floss.

## YARN

One of the most satisfying aspects of doing needlepoint is choosing, handling and working with the yarns available in department and needlework stores. Wool is the most commonly used yarn because of its versatility and long-wearing qualities. It covers the canvas completely when worked up, forming even, plump stitches. Most needlepoint wool is colorfast and permanently mothproofed. Make sure yours is both.

Spurred on by the renaissance of all kinds of embroidery, many manufacturers have made recent advances to improve the quality, durability and color range of wool yarns. Also, the list of manufacturers who produce the "raw materials" of canvas embroidery has expanded from two or three to almost a dozen in the last few years.

The finest wool to work over canvas is Persian wool, manufactured under several brand names including Paternayan, Paragon and Bon Pasteur. It is spun from long smooth fibers and is soft and lustrous. The threads are composed of three loosely twisted strands, which can be used together or singly. This wool is sold by the ounce (about 45 threads), by 4-ounce or 8-ounce skeins and by the pound. Some stores even sell single threads. You will soon discover that Persian yarns come in a dizzying array of colors.

In some cases, you will want to switch to crewel wools, which may be necessary for work on very fine gauge canvas. Crewel wools are similar to Persian wools, but they are thinner. This yarn comes in 20- to 25-yard skeins and is composed of two loosely twisted strands which can be used together or separately.

Wool tapestry yarn is available in most stores that sell Persian and crewel yarns. The four plies that form one thread are tightly twisted and cannot be separated, making this type of yarn less versatile than the others. Tapestry yarn is best suited for use on pieces on which you will be working stitches that require the same thickness of thread; for instance, the Florentine stitches. Traditionally, tapestry yarn has been used to work a design solely in Tent over a 10 count Penelope canvas. These yarns do not have quite the color range or brilliance found in Persian yarns. However, the general quality has been improved greatly in the last few years, and you will find this a good material to work with. It is sold in 8 to 9 yard and 40-yard skeins.

Rug wool is used on 3 and 5 count canvases. It is very thick yarn and comes in a wide range of colors. While you can separate the three plies making up each thread, they become kinky and unmanageable. Therefore, you should work only with a full thread. Rug wool is sold by the pound; there are about 225 yards per pound. It should be noted that three full Persian threads are equivalent to one thread of rug yarn in thickness. Because of this it is possible to interchange Persian for rug wool when a small amount is needed.

Knitting wools are not very successful materials to work over canvas. The yarns are spun from short fibered wool, which tends to fuzz easily and wear out more quickly when pulled through canvas. In addition, the colors are not as vibrant and clear as those associated with Persian yarns.

Although wool yarns may be the stuff of life in canvas embroidery, some of the following materials must certainly be the spice! Do not hesitate to experiment with different kinds of thread for added texture and various special effects.

Mercerized cotton or linen embroidery floss gives added sheen to finished pieces and is excellent to use for highlighting. Also, it can be used as the main material over fine gauge canvas for fairly small projects. The strands are thin and may have to be doubled up or "tripled up" in the needle to achieve the desired thickness.

Silk threads are generally expensive imports, which add luxurious sparkle to a piece. An iridescent effect can be added by stitching with three different colors of silk thread at the same time. While the looks that silk create are attractive, the material itself is hard to work with. The threads are delicate and fragile and must be worked with in short lengths. In addition, anyone with even a mild case of dishpan hands should forget about stitching with silk, as the threads will snag and catch, the individual filaments pulling loose and "giving up"! Some people have found that running silk threads through beeswax makes them easier to handle.

Stitching with metal threads has been done for centuries, especially in ecclesiastical work. However, there are many other possibilities for using metal threads outside church pieces. (Consider introducing gold and silver threads into a formal purse, for instance.) Areas of metal thread stitching should be traméed or understitched with wool, cotton or silk. The intensity and quality of the resulting shimmer will be determined by the color and thickness of the thread underneath.

Two kinds of metal threads suitable for canvas work.

There are various kinds of metallic threads available, some being quite expensive and considered a luxury item. Whatever kind you get, make sure it is tarnish-proof. If the strands, which can be doubled or tripled in the needle to the proper thickness, tend to snag and twist, you can drag the threads through beeswax before stitching with them. (To remove the wax, press the finished piece facedown on a clean cloth.)

## FOUND MATERIALS

British needlewomen, especially, have made great use of "found" materials to ornament their embroidery. Found materials are any treasures you have collected, such as beads, shells, sequins or smoothed-down glass. Any of these items can be used to enhance your finished work. However, they should be planned for as an integral part of the design while the project is in progress and not added as an afterthought, or they will look "pasted on." Make sure whatever found object you use in your work is waterproof, color-fast and tarnishproof.

Found materials can add a decorative touch to your work. However, be sure they are not put on as an afterthought.

## NEEDLES

Needlepoint or tapestry needles have large eyes and blunt points. They are available in several sizes: sizes 22–24 for petit point canvas, sizes 17–20 for gros point canvas, and sizes 13–15 for quick point (rug) canvas. In other words, the higher the number, the finer and more pointed the needle will be. The lower its number, the longer, thicker and blunter it will be.

The needle you choose to work with will be determined by the gauge of the canvas and the thickness of the yarn. Too large a needle will unthread easily and will be difficult to pull through the canvas. Too small a needle will be almost impossible to thread and will wear thin spots in the yarn.

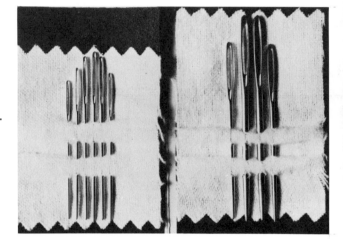

Tapestry needles of various sizes.

You should be able to thread the needle with ease. At the same time, the needle should move through the canvas holes without the slightest resistance. A number 18 needle is the best general purpose size for most kinds of work. A number 13 is good for working thick yarn on rug canvas, and a number 22 is best for very fine work.

Do not think your needles are ruined if they become discolored and lose their smooth surface, making them difficult to pull through the canvas. This condition usually is due to oxidation, and it can be corrected if you periodically run your needles through a sand-filled pincushion.

Some people are allergic to steel needles. If you notice that your fingers become excessively sore while stitching, have a jeweler gold-plate your needles, or dip them frequently in clear nail polish to alleviate the problem.

## SCISSORS

Two pairs of scissors are useful for canvas work. Keep on hand a large heavy-duty type for cutting canvas and skeins of yarn and a small, sharp-pointed pair for cutting the tails of yarn as you work the canvas piece.

## THIMBLES

The use of a thimble is optional and a matter of personal preference. If you are comfortable with one, by all means use it. The middle finger and forefinger can become quite chapped and sore from concentrated work sessions, and a thimble is good preventive medicine.

## FRAMES

Some people make use of embroidery frames for working needlepoint, especially large, bulky pieces such as rugs. The use of a frame impedes easy swinging and canvas rotating to a certain extent, and, therefore, the use of a frame may become more a hindrance than a help. Persons with a manual handicap may find that a frame is a necessity for working needlepoint.

When possible, a frame without a stand should be used, as this will enable the worker to rotate the needlepoint piece just by turning the frame around.

## STORING YOUR SUPPLIES

It is important to take good care of all your needlepoint supplies and to keep them in order. This will assure that your materials will be clean and easily accessible when you are ready to use them.

Extra needles can be stored in a needle case, tips down in a cork, in the original package or small pill bottle. Do not leave needles pinned through the canvas. Invariably they will come loose, and you will have to launch a frantic search to make sure the missing needle was not retrieved by your children or the family pet. If you want to have a few needles on hand, pin

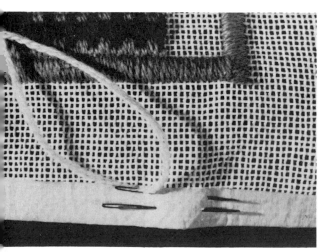

If you want extra needles on hand, leave them pinned through the canvas hem or tape.

them through the taped or hemmed edge of the canvas. The tape or fabric will prevent them from slipping through.

The nicest way to store your small scissors is to make a needlepoint case for them. If they are not kept in a case, the points should be stuck into a cork to protect them *and* your fingers.

Yarn *always* should be tied loosely in the middle to keep the strands from getting into a hopeless tangle. Remember, the more you have to pull at the yarn to separate strands, the more it will wear. The loosely tied bunches should be stored in plastic bags to keep them clean and dry.

If you have a lot of extra yarn, it is a good idea to organize the bunches by color family. The yarn can be stored by slipping a shower hook through the knots. These groups are placed in plastic bags. Or the bunches can be tied to a coat hanger, placed under a plastic cover and hung in a closet.

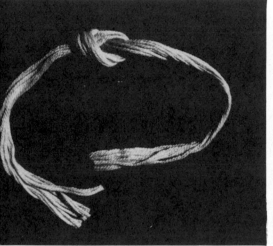

Keep bunches of yarn loosely knotted to avoid tangling.

Extra yarn can be stored on old shower hooks in color groups.

Another way to store extra yarn is to knot the bunches over a coat hanger. Cover with a plastic bag and hang in a closet.

A yarn caddy with project in the works.　　　　　The yarn caddy tied closed with cording.

## MAKE YOUR OWN YARN CADDY

A yarn caddy is a portable, safe and attractive way to store your needlepoint project now in progress. The loops of yarn are slipped through slots in the center fabric panel, the folded canvas is laid flat down on top, and then the caddy is rolled like a newspaper and tied closed.

1. Cut 2 pieces of fabric 15″ x 25″; one is the "fashion fabric" and the other is a sturdy lining. Cut a piece of the lining fabric 6½″ x 25″ for the center panel.

2. On the center panel, turn under a ¼″ hem on top and bottom and top-stitch by machine.

3. Make a "sandwich" with the fashion fabric face up, then the center panel face down and then the lining face down. Pin the sandwich together to keep the pieces from slipping. Stitch around 3 sides about ¼″ in from the edge. Leave one end open. Clip the corners and press the seams open.

4. Turn the sandwich right side out and press flat. Pin two 25″ lengths of cording looped in half at the seam between the fashion and lining fabrics. Tuck under the raw fabric edges.

5. Topstitch the fourth side closed through all layers and continue top-stitching around the other 3 sides for a finished look.

6. Stitch vertical lines at about 2″ intervals down the center panel through all thicknesses.

A twist of wire or knitting-stitch holder can be used to slip the yarn through the center panel slots. Also, extra pockets and slots can be made in the caddy for storing needles, scissors and thimbles.

Use a knitting stitch holder to pull the yarn through the center panel slots of the caddy.

A clamp style report fastener can be used for rolling sections of the canvas out of the way while you are working.

## HOW TO HANDLE THE CANVAS

Needlepoint canvas is apt to be quite stiff when first cut due to the sizing added to keep the vertical and horizontal threads or mesh in place. This stiffness, which indicates high quality merchandise, may cause the early stitching to be somewhat cumbersome and awkward. Don't be afraid to work with the canvas to loosen it up and make it more pliable. The blocking process will restore the original body and shape the canvas had before stitching.

If you are right-handed, it generally is a good idea to work the piece from right to left and from top to bottom, as this will keep the bulky, worked sections out of your free hand. Left-handed people should work their pieces in the opposite order, from left to right and bottom to top. Keep the thumb of your free hand on the surface of the canvas to help guide the needle and to smooth down the stitches as you work.

Many people like to roll the canvas up to keep the bulkier sections out of the way. If you decide to try this, be very careful not to catch up previously worked areas in the new stitching. You can purchase (for well under a dollar) two plastic clamp-style report fasteners which are obtainable at any office supply store. Slip these "rods" over the side edges of the canvas, roll the unwanted sections around them like a scroll, and pin in place. This is a comfortable, "safe" way to work.

Many people mark the top of the canvas to eliminate the chance of accidentally stitching some sections sideways. It is advisable to set up your design with the selvage at the right or left side.

## ROTATING THE CANVAS

When working most canvas stitches you will find that the work goes faster and is easier if you turn the canvas around 180° (top to bottom and bottom to top) at the completion of each row. Rotating the canvas in no way changes the stitch patterns. There are a few exceptions to this rule, and these are noted in the stitch write-ups in Chapter 3.

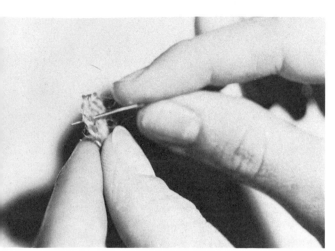
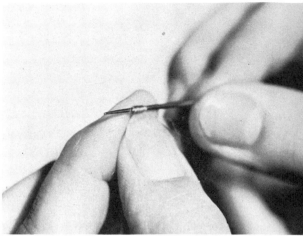

## THREADING THE NEEDLE

Many people have given up on canvas embroidery because they have not gotten past threading the needle! It is virtually impossible to thread a tapestry needle with Persian yarn in the normal fashion. There is a trick to it. Loop a small section of thread over the needle and squeeze it tightly between your thumb and index finger. Slip the needle out and line up the top of the loop with the eye of the needle, still holding the loop tightly between your thumb and forefinger. Then, gently push or "rock" the yarn through the eye and pull on the loop until the tail comes out. Slide the needle slowly along the thread until the tail is 8″ or 10″ long. If the strands of yarn you are using have separated, retwist them loosely before threading.

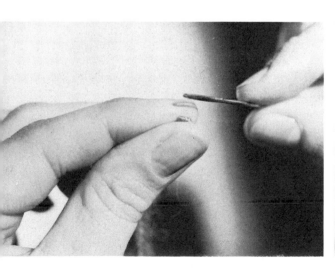
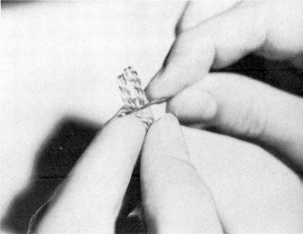

## BEGINNING AND ENDING THREADS

There are a number of ways to secure the beginning of a new thread. You can come through from the back of the canvas at 1 (see numbering on diagrams), leaving about a 1″ long tail on the wrong side. Hold this tail against the canvas back and work so that the understitching "pins" the tail to the canvas.

When a worked area is established, the beginning tail of new threads can be woven through an inch of previous work on the back side of the canvas. This will hold them securely in place.

Some people knot the end of the thread and pass the threaded needle from front to back an inch or so into the margin adjacent to the area to be worked, thus leaving the knot on the surface of the canvas. The tail is pinned down with understitching, and the knotted end is cut off later. There *never* should be any knots in a finished piece of needlepoint.

Secure the beginning or end of a thread by running it under previously worked stitches on the back of the canvas.

The tails of yarn should be cut closer. This is a messy canvas backing!

To complete a thread, weave it through an inch of understitching on the back side of the canvas, and then trim off the excess tail to within ½″ of the work. It is important to keep the back of your work neat to avoid snagging and to make it possible to apply press-on Pellon if needed in the mounting process after the piece is worked.

Never run colored strands under white or any other light color when beginning or ending threads. This may show through, giving the appearance that the colors have bled.

Often in working designs, small amounts of one color may be used in several scattered areas, and you will find it time-consuming and wasteful to end and begin the yarn with each move. You can "carry" the yarn across the back of the canvas to the new area, but do not allow more than ½″ of yarn to be exposed, or it may snag and get caught in subsequent stitching. When carrying a thread more than ½″, weave it under previously worked stitches and do not pull it too tightly.

Avoid piercing the canvas mesh with the needle while working. This can cause the yarn to get caught, and it weakens the canvas.

The tails of yarn are cut close here, preventing possible snagging.

## USE OF LEFTOVER SINGLE STRANDS

In the course of working a stitch in double strands, you may find that you have collected a few odd single strands of yarn. The following is a little trick in "yarn economy."

Double up the strand and thread the *ends* through the needle. Bring the needle and yarn from back to front at 1 on the stitch diagram in chapter 3, holding the loop at the back. Go to the back at 2, pass the needle through the loop, and come out at 3. Presto! The new strand has been secured with minimal wastage, since weaving under wasn't necessary.

## WORKING WITH MORE THAN ONE THREADED NEEDLE

There will be many times when you will be working alternately with two or more colors. The best way to avoid tangling and snagging is to pull the threaded needles you are not using at the moment through to the right side of the canvas. Secure these needles out of the way, making sure the full length of yarn is on the surface of the canvas where you can keep an eye on it. This method of working conserves yarn because you will not be beginning and ending strands each time a different color comes up.

## SWINGING

"Swing" is a term given to the rhythmical motion of working whereby one stitch is completed and the next stitch is begun all in one motion. After bringing the needle and full length of yarn through to the front of the canvas at 1 on the diagram, you will slip the needle to the back of the canvas at 2 and out again at 3. Then pull the yarn through again.

Never pull the yarn all the way out at the back of the canvas, then through at the front and again at the back in separate steps. This "poking" will result in uneven tension and lots of wasted motion. Swinging to the beginning of each new stitch and working with the yarn at the front of the canvas is accurate, speedy, relaxing and makes for beautiful, even work.

## TENSION

Tension—how tightly or loosely you stitch—is a major factor in the appearance of your finished work. Uniformity is important. The yarn should be pulled smoothly and consistently, not so loose that the stitches look lumpy nor so tight that they pull the canvas out of shape.

The tension of this stitching is too tight. The canvas is pulling out of shape.

The tension here is too loose, creating lumpy, uneven stitches.

The tension of this stitching is good; the canvas has maintained its shape, and the stitches cover the canvas adequately.

If you discover a place in the finished work where the stitches appear to be too tight or too loose, correct it as best you can. Loose stitches can be tightened by pulling the thread on the wrong side of the canvas with the needle. Tight stitches can be "plumped up" with the needle on the right side of the canvas. These defects can be avoided if you check the tension as you stitch, tightening and "plumping" as necessary.

Each person develops a personal rhythm and tension of stitching once the stitches are learned, and swinging from the end of one stitch to the beginning of the next becomes automatic. Proper swinging is the most important single factor in achieving even tension.

## YARN COUNT

How much yarn to buy is one of the first and most troublesome questions that comes up at the beginning of each new needlepoint project. People worry, and rightly, that they will be unable to match dye lots if they buy "short." At the same time, they don't want to spend money for yarn that will be left over. As a general rule, it is always better to buy too much—the extra yarn in combination with other leftovers may inspire a whole new project.

Yarn requirements are influenced by several factors—the number of colors to be used; the specific stitches to be worked; the type, length, thickness and color of the yarn; individual techniques of application and the gauge and dimensions of the canvas.

To be generous, usually figure on two full strands of wool per square inch of worked area (on 14 count canvas). For large areas, multiply the length by the width to determine the number of square inches to be worked. Then multiply this figure by two to get an approximation of how many strands you will need to complete the piece.

Your thumb is a good guide for figuring the number of square inches to be worked in small areas. The "fingerprint area" of the thumb is about 1 square inch. If you still are uncertain, work a square inch of the stitch in question in the blank canvas margin.

An exact yarn count per square inch is included in each write-up in the chapter on stitches to assist you in figuring out yarn requirements. These counts have been calculated for 14 count canvas; the same stitch worked on a different gauge canvas would require a different amount of yarn. Keep in mind that you will buy *less* yarn if working with stitches that do not require a full strand to cover the canvas.

## CHOOSING COLORS

Try to get a fairly firm notion of the colors you want to use in a project before you go to make your selection of yarns. If you are doing an abstract or simple design, you probably will not need to purchase several shades of each color. However, if you are doing a design that requires modeling, you will need several shades to create a realistic appearance.

Remember when looking through the hundreds of colors that they look brighter in skeins on a shelf than they will worked into stitches over your canvas. The colors tend to darken very slightly due to the tiny shadows that are cast between each stitch.

If possible, select your colors by putting skeins together rather than trying to pick colors from a yarn sample card or from small swatches. You can get a much better idea of how the colors are going to work together when you can see and move around large areas of the colors. Also, look at the colors in daylight. Indoor fluorescent lighting distorts yarn colors as much as it distorts the color of clothing.

Black tends to look harsh when used with many of the soft yarn colors. Therefore, if you want to use black but don't want it to stick out, use navy blue or charcoal gray instead. When worked up, these colors "read" black. However, they are softer and won't interfere with your other yarn colors.

You can find additional notes on color in Chapter 4.

## HANDLING THE YARN

Many people wonder what length strands of yarn they should use for canvas embroidery. In most cases, a strand approximately 30″ long will do nicely. This is the length obtained when a skein of yarn is opened out into a long "tube," then cut at each end to form two bunches of yarn. Using shorter than 30″ strands will mean a lot of unnecessary stopping and starting.

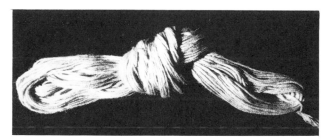

A skein of yarn, uncut.

The skein opened out into a tube.

Cutting the skein into two even bunches.

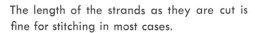

The length of the strands as they are cut is fine for stitching in most cases.

Keep in mind that the yarn you are working with is taking a lot of abuse as it is repeatedly pulled through the canvas. The longer the strand of yarn, the more times it will be pulled through, and the more tiny fibers will be worn off. Be alert to thin places that may develop in your work from using worn yarn. End the strand and begin a new one. If you are using especially thick or short-fibered yarn, work with shorter lengths. Also, you can slide the needle to a new location on the strand every so often to keep the eye from wearing through one spot.

If you hold a strand of wool up to a strong light, you will discover that the fibers radiate from the central stem mostly in one direction, either up or down. This is the direction in which the fibers were spun into strands. Another test to determine which way the fibers go is to pull a strand through your fingers. If you are pulling the strand "with the grain," the fuzzy ends will lie in close to the strand. If you are pulling "against the grain," the ends will flare out.

A real refinement to your work is to thread the needle so that the fiber ends will be smoothed down as you stitch. (The ends should point downward away from the needle.) This procedure will give you maximum use of your yarn strands and a fine evenness to the finished stitches.

Sometimes as you work you will notice that the yarn becomes twisted and snags easily. This is especially true when working the diagonal stitches. This problem can be remedied by letting the yarn and needle dangle freely from the canvas; the yarn will unwind by itself.

## THIN PLACES AND TRAMÉ

Thin places in the worked stitches or places where the canvas shows through result from using too few strands or worn wool, using very dark colors on white canvas or having too tight a tension. If thin or frayed places do occur, restitching in the same color with a single strand directly on top of the old stitches will usually correct the problem.

Some thin places can be eliminated by the use of a technique called "tramé." In this process, single, double or full strands of yarn are worked in long horizontal stitches on the canvas. The regular stitching is done over this "grounding." If a thin place is discovered after the work is finished, the tramé threads can be woven underneath afterward. Also, you can tramé an area before stitching as preventive medicine or as a color guide.

Tramé can be used to create beautiful effects. Some of the most exquisite ancient ecclesiastical work made use of delicately hued silk tramé threads overstitched with gold or silver. These pieces seem to shimmer, and a hint of the tramé thread color glows through the top stitching. This basic concept can be applied effectively to modern pieces using matching yarns or special threads.

## RIPPING OUT WORN YARN AND ERRORS

If you discover an error in your work, it is best to remove it before you go any further. Even though the process of ripping out errors is annoying and tedious, the finished piece will suffer if the errors are allowed to remain. Content yourself with the knowledge that it is easier to correct now than after the bad section is surrounded by other work.

Do not try to poke the threaded needle back through the canvas to "unstitch," as inevitably you will catch and snag yarn on the underside, creating an even worse situation. Remove the yarn from the needle and use the point of the needle to pick out the unwanted stitches, one by one. Fuzzy ends that have worked through to the surface should be picked out from the back of the canvas. Picked-out yarn tends to be thin and kinky and should not be reused.

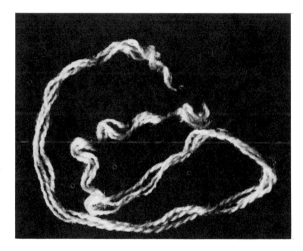

Do not try to reuse picked-out wool as it tends to wear thin and snag.

There are occasions when small, pointed scissors or a seam-ripper will be the most efficient tool for removing a bad section. When using these implements, be very careful not to cut the canvas underneath the stitches being taken out. Secure remaining loose yarn ends on the underside of the canvas after ripping or picking out.

## REPAIRING TORN OR CUT CANVAS

Occasionally a mesh of the canvas is accidentally severed while ripping out errors. It may be possible to glue a single cut mesh in place or to cover it over with yarn. However, the most successful approach is to snip a section of mesh out of the margin of the canvas. Place this under the damaged area carefully matching up the mesh. Needlepoint through both layers. There is virtually no added bulk where two layers of mesh fall together, and after the area is worked, the error will be invisible. Areas of canvas that have been

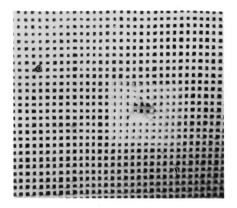

Cut a patch of canvas from the margin to repair a cut or torn section.

Place the new patch under the damaged area and stitch through both layers.

chewed by the family pet or otherwise injured can be patched according to the above method, using as large a section of new canvas mesh as is needed.

## THE IMPORTANCE OF USING COLORFAST MATERIALS

All the materials and canvas design markings in your needlepoint pieces must be colorfast. After a piece is completed, it usually is blocked to restore body and the original shape before the piece is mounted. The process of blocking involves steaming or wetting the piece. If the threads or underneath design are not colorfast, bleeding into other colors or the background may occur. Once a color has run, a whole section may have to be replaced, or worse, the entire piece may be ruined. Most types of thread sold for needlework are colorfast, but it is a good idea to double check the label. If you have yarn you want to use but aren't sure if it is colorfast, put a strand in a bowl of water overnight and see if it runs. Be especially suspicious of "unknown" reds, blues and blacks.

Paints or markers with which you are unfamiliar should be patch tested before you commit the canvas and stitching to them. Apply some color to a spare scrap of canvas and wait until it is thoroughly dry. Then wet it and rub a little. If it smears or runs, don't use it!

## KEEPING YOUR WORK CLEAN

You should hear the cries of dismay from professional blockers and mounters when they get in a piece that is smudged and spotted! Many times people will read the newspaper and then start to stitch, unknowingly working the ink into the yarn as they go along. This is particularly noticeable with light colors.

Obviously, some stains and smudging are accidental. You can't count on your work receiving tender treatment from your curious children and dog. When a spot is discovered, it can be worked on with a small amount of Woolite and a damp cloth. Do not use a detergent. Or, you can try using a spot remover such as K2r or Goddards.

The main thing is to practice preventive medicine. Wash your hands before each work session. This is a must. Keeping your work properly stored will eliminate many chance encounters with peanut butter and muddy paws. Finally, Scotch-gard pieces that will receive a lot of wear.

Pieces that have been in use for months and years will need dry cleaning at some point. Heritage pieces can be reblocked and cleaned, and they will look as good as new. Make sure your cleaner is experienced with this kind of work before entrusting it to him. The cleaning process will probably remove some of the sizing from the piece. You can restiffen the piece by spraying the back with sizing after the work has been cleaned.

Keeping your work properly stored will eliminate the chance that Rover will choose your latest project as a plaything.

"Who, me?"

# CHAPTER 3

# Stitches

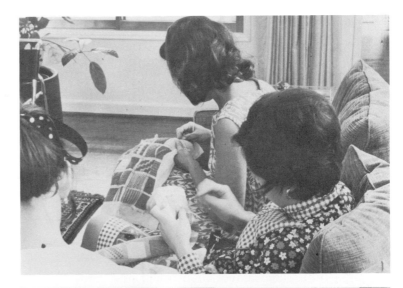

## INTRODUCTION

Each stitch included in this chapter creates a unique pattern and texture when worked on canvas. Some of the stitches have been used for centuries in needlepoint. Others have been adapted at some point in time from crewel embroidery. An attempt has been made to include examples of many kinds of canvas stitches.

One section is devoted to several Florentine stitch patterns with some information on their background. Another section deals with overlaid stitches that add an extra decorative touch to finished needlepoint. Some stitch variations are presented at the end of the chapter.

No canvas stitch is difficult to work once you have mastered its particular count. You should practice each stitch before using it in a project; making a sampler is the best way to learn the stitches. This provides you with a permanent and handy record of their appearance.

This chapter has been organized according to natural stitch groupings and the order in which the stitches are worked. The sequence of stitching presented here has been developed for comfort, ease and speed and has been used successfully by hundreds of students and accomplished needle-pointers. However, you may find in other sources that the same stitch is presented in a different order. There is no absolute "right way" to work a stitch as long as you are consistent in the order you choose.

You may know a stitch by another name; some of the stitches have several names, adding to the confusion. Wherever possible, alternate stitch names have been included in the write-ups.

Left-handed stitchers have received very little attention in regard to what order they should follow when working canvas stitches. Hopefully, all "southpaws" will find a solution to the problem in this chapter.

Each stitch is described in detail with color suggestions and suggestions for its use in projects. The stitch is illustrated photographically to show the appearance of a finished area. Also, it is shown schematically in diagrams to help you learn exactly how the stitch is worked on canvas.

## COMPENSATING STITCHES

Many of the canvas stitches in this section require partial stitch units to fill out a worked area or tiny patches of uncovered canvas would show through, detracting from the appearance of the finished piece. These filler or "cheat" units are referred to as "compensating stitches." They are designed to fit in unobtrusively with the main stitch pattern.

## STITCH BACKING

The term "backing" refers to the pattern created by a given stitch on the wrong side of the canvas. Some of the stitch backings are tight and firm while others are practically nonexistent. You should avoid using stitches with little or weak backings for projects that will get a great deal of hard use.

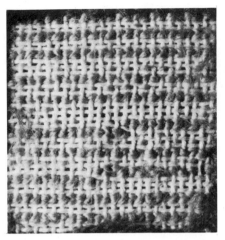

This is a weak stitch backing.

## NUMBER OF COLORS

The color possibilities in canvas embroidery are virtually limitless. However, some stitches with strong texture are particularly effective when worked in one color, such as Old Florentine, Oblong with Backstitch and Italian Cross. Other stitches are most effective when worked in two or more colors, such as Interwoven Herringbone and Crossed Corners. Still other stitches are effective when worked in shaded areas. The Florentine stitches are a good example.

Mixing different colored strands in the needle and working them simultaneously can create very subtle shading if the colors are closely related. If the colors are not alike, a tweedy look will result.

Color treatment suggestions for each stitch have been included as a general guide in the write-ups.

## STRAND COUNT

The discussions in this chapter assume the use of 3-ply Persian wool. Needlepoint stitches vary in the thickness of wool needed to adequately cover the canvas. Each diagram suggests the use of a full, double or single strand of yarn.

The decision to use a full, double or single strand of yarn is determined by how adequately the canvas is being covered, and this in turn depends on the canvas gauge, the stitch and the quality of yarn you are using. Some-

Too few strands are being used to cover the canvas adequately.

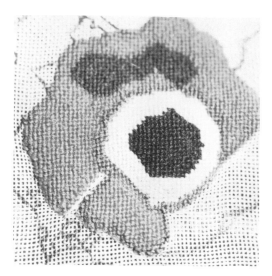

This is too much yarn for the gauge canvas being worked. Note how the canvas is pulling out of shape.

times yarn thickness varies from color to color and from one dye lot to another, so experimenting may be necessary to achieve good canvas coverage.

The allotments listed in this chapter have been calculated for 14 count mono canvas. The same stitches worked over a finer or coarser canvas would require fewer or more strands.

## MESH COUNT

All canvas stitches follow definite counted patterns; each one is worked over a prescribed number of vertical and/or horizontal canvas mesh. In analyzing the stitch diagrams, always count mesh, and *never* count holes.

The diagrams in this section give suggested pattern counts with occasional variations. For example, Gobelin Droit (page 50) has a 3-0-1 count. This means that you will cross 3 horizontal mesh and no (0) vertical mesh to form the stitch. The "1" at the end of the sequence indicates the number of vertical mesh between each stitch. These mesh counts are intended as guides in helping you set up the various stitch patterns.

The counts have been abbreviated where several steps make up the stitch pattern. For instance, Hungarian stitch (page 57) actually is worked over a 2-0-1, 4-0-1, 2-0-2 count. However, this has been shortened to a 2-4-2 count in the write up to eliminate having to decipher a long list of numbers. The numbers here indicate that the first stitch is worked over a 2 count, the second over 4 and the third over 2.

## IF YOU'RE LEFT-HANDED

The stitch diagrams in this book are oriented for right-handed people. However, do not despair of figuring out the stitches and working them! You will work in the reverse order shown in the diagrams. Therefore, you will work "right to left" stitches from left to right. Diagonal stitches that begin in the upper left for right-handed people will begin in the lower right for you. Turning the book upside down is a help in learning these stitches.

If you find that working the diagonal stitches from lower right to upper left is uncomfortable, you might try turning the diagrams sideways, beginning your stitching in the lower left corner and working to upper right. Some left-handed students have found this stitching sequence more satisfactory than reversing the order completely.

If you're still having trouble conquering a new stitch, trace the diagram on thin tracing paper and turn the tracing over. Now add *your* numbering sequence, and everything should become clear. See Stitch 1 (page 44) for special instructions on learning Diagonal Tent.

## DIAGRAM NUMBERING AND COLORS

All of the diagrams in this chapter are numbered to indicate the sequence and direction of stitching. Odd numbers represent the beginning of a stitch; the needle comes through from the back to the front of the canvas at this point. Even numbers represent the end of a stitch; here the needle goes from the front of the canvas to the back.

You will notice that some of the numbers on the diagrams are upside down. This means that the canvas has been rotated for the second row, and you are now working with the canvas turned around with top at bottom and bottom at top.

Many of the diagrams indicate the use of more than one color in working the stitch. Note when reading the diagrams that BLACK represents the first color and/or operation, and the CROSS-HATCH screen represents the second color and/or operation. The STRIPED screen represents compensating stitches for both the first and second colors.

# 1

## DIAGONAL TENT
*(Petit Point, Gros Point, Half
Cross, or Continental)*

1¾ double strands = 1 sq. in.
1 color
1-1-2 count
do not rotate canvas

The Tent stitch has been used so extensively in canvas embroidery from the earliest times that many people have the mistaken idea that this is the *only* canvas stitch. Although, as you will see, there are dozens of stitches that can be worked on canvas, it can be said that Tent is one of the most versatile, durable and well-liked canvas stitches. A good rule of thumb is: When in doubt, use Tent!

This stitch, which slants up and to the right, crossing the intersection of 1 horizontal and 1 vertical mesh, has been called by many names. When worked over small gauge canvas, it sometimes is called Petit Point, and over large gauge canvas, Gros Point. Another name, Half Cross, is descriptive of the stitch's appearance.

Tent worked over Penelope canvas with fine detail worked with the canvas mesh separated to form areas of half-size mono canvas.

Tent worked on 40 count gauze with one strand of embroidery floss. Ann Gaudineer, Des Moines. Designed by Jean McIntosh.

Some people will recognize Tent under the name Continental. This refers to the stitch when it is worked in horizontal rows across the canvas. This method probably was devised when working the stitch over tramé threads. The disadvantages of the method are so great that these authors do not even teach it and discourage the use of Continental altogether, except for very small areas or outlining.

First of all, Continental pulls the canvas badly out of shape and causes it to roll, sometimes to the extent that blocking cannot fully restore the original shape of the worked piece. In addition, stitching by this method creates ridges and inconsistencies which detract from the smooth, even effect of a finished section of Tent. Also, the backing stitch pattern on the reverse side of the canvas is not strong with Continental, and this shortens the lifespan of the piece.

Continental backing pattern.

The name to learn and remember is Diagonal Tent or Basketweave. Here, the stitches are worked on the diagonal grain of the canvas, and the rows dovetail together with regularity and smoothness. The finished work calls to mind strands of tiny pearls all lined up or a perfect ear of corn. The stitch pattern on the reverse side of the canvas is very strong and looks woven, giving rise to the name Basketweave.

Basketweave backing pattern.

The actual process of stitching Diagonal Tent is relaxing because of the rhythm and swing of the needle. The end result is superior in consistency, and the worker will delight to see the canvas looking more like a rectangle than a parallelogram! Those who are accustomed to working Continental may experience momentary difficulty in changing over to Diagonal Tent, but once they have learned it, they will *never* wish to return to the old method. Beginners will be surprised to see how professional their initial efforts at needlepoint can look when working Diagonal Tent, and for the experienced "Basketweavers" there is a refinement presented here that will be of special interest.

If Diagonal Tent is new to you, it will be easiest for you to mark off a *square* on the canvas for experimenting. Begin in the lower right corner of the area you are planning to cover, as this will give you a chance to make a long row before having to turn to start a new row.

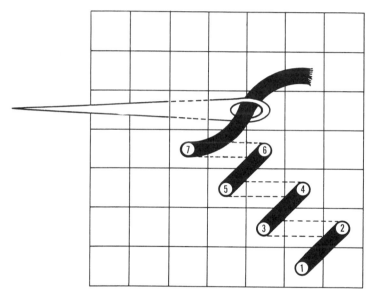

Beginning in this corner, perform the stitch by crossing 1 intersection, moving up over a horizontal mesh and to the right over a vertical mesh. Without pulling your needle and thread through to the back, swing the needle straight *across* to the left under 2 vertical mesh to the new hole and then pull the thread through to the front. You will be ending one stitch and beginning the next in the same motion. Repeat the operation, and shortly, a diagonal line of stitches going from lower right to upper left will result.

Now it is time to change direction. You will make a "turning" stitch and start the next row at the side of the canvas. Swing the needle to the hole directly below the *bottom* of the last stitch and pull the thread through to the front. You are starting a "down" row and have not needed to rotate the canvas.

The stitch is still the same count, going up to the right over 1 intersection. Swing your needle straight *down* under 2 horizontal mesh to the new hole.

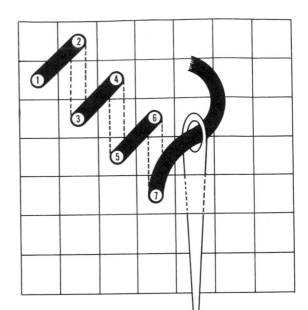

Pull the thread through to the front and repeat. Continue going down until you come to the bottom boundary. To change direction here, start the turning stitch directly to the *left* of the *bottom* of the last stitch and head up again, finding each new hole by swinging straight across to the left under 2 vertical mesh. You will notice that the rows interlock and that you are creating a basketweave pattern on the back of the canvas.

The main points to remember are:

1. The stitch itself slants up and to the right crossing a vertical and a horizontal mesh, or 1 intersection.

2. When working an ascending or "up" row, swing the needle straight *across* to the left under 2 vertical mesh from where you completed the last stitch to find the starting hole for the next stitch.

3. When working a descending or "down" row, swing the needle straight *down* under 2 horizontal mesh to find the hole for the next stitch.

4. To change direction at the top or bottom boundary, start a stitch directly to the *left* of the bottom of the previous stitch.

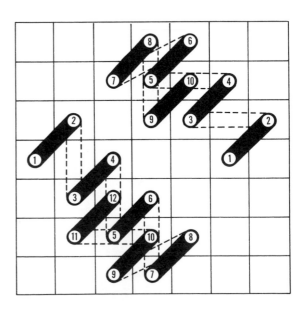

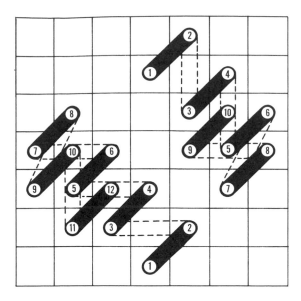

5. To change direction at either side boundary, start a stitch directly *below* the bottom of the previous stitch.

6. (Once you have mastered the stitching method, it will be easier and best to consistently begin work in the upper right corner of the area you plan to cover. Never rotate the canvas for Diagonal Tent.)

Remember that the canvas is a fabric created by the even weaving together of warp (vertical) and weft (horizontal) threads. Upon close examination, you will notice, following the natural grain of the canvas, that the intersections alternate between having the horizontal mesh and the vertical mesh on top. Now look at the intersections following the diagonal grain of the canvas. Instead of alternating, a whole diagonal row will have the horizontal mesh on top at the intersections, and the adjacent rows will have the vertical mesh on top at the intersections.

The authors have found that almost every flaw in the final appearance of the work can be eliminated if you are careful to be consistent in covering vertical mesh intersections on "down" rows and horizontal mesh intersections

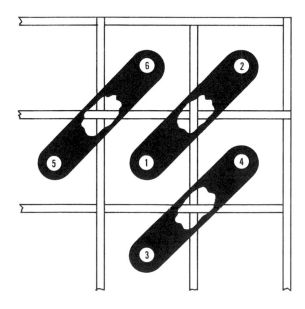

on "up" rows. There is no guesswork as to whether you will proceed up or down. If a vertical mesh is on top at the intersection, you always will start a "down" row, and if a horizontal mesh is on top at the intersection, you always will start an "up" row.

This is particularly useful when you are working areas that don't touch. You can be sure, no matter how scattered the worked areas are, that the final work will fit together as perfectly and neatly as the pieces of a puzzle, and the natural weave of the underlying canvas will be minimally disturbed.

*For Left-Handed Workers:* Mark off a square on your canvas for experimenting and begin your work in the upper left corner. You will go down over a horizontal mesh and to the left over a vertical mesh crossing 1 intersection. When working a "down" row, swing the needle straight *across* to the right under 2 vertical mesh from where you completed the last stitch to the next free hole. When working an "up" row, swing the needle straight *up* under 2 horizontal mesh to the new hole.

To turn at the top or bottom boundaries, start a stitch directly to the *right* of the top of the previous stitch. To turn at the side boundaries, start a stitch directly *above* the top of the previous stitch. Once you have mastered the method, begin your work in the lower left corner of the area you plan to cover. Note which mesh is on top at the intersection you are crossing. If it is a vertical mesh, you always will start an "up" row, and if it is a horizontal mesh, you always will start a "down" row.

Your instructions are the reverse of those for right-handed people. Now *turn the book upside down* and examine all the diagrams for Diagonal Tent. This will show you exactly how to proceed.

## 2

## GOBELIN DROIT

*(Upright or Straight Gobelin,*
*or Satin)*

1 full strand = 1 sq. in.
1 color, shade or stripe
3-0-1 count
rotate canvas

Gobelin Droit is a very old stitch that forms upright ridges in imitation of tapestry. It can be worked up quickly, is suitable for background or filler and has a strong backing.

The stitch is worked from right to left, rotating the canvas for each row. It can be worked over a count of 2-0-1, 3-0-1 or 4-0-1. Be careful to maintain a uniform tension and to avoid twisting the yarn while working. This stitch has a tendency to show canvas between rows if pulled too tightly.

You can use one or more colors to achieve a shaded or striped effect. A Backstitch can be worked between the rows for decoration and to cover the canvas. A contrasting thread can be run beneath the stitches. When this is done, the stitch is called Renaissance.

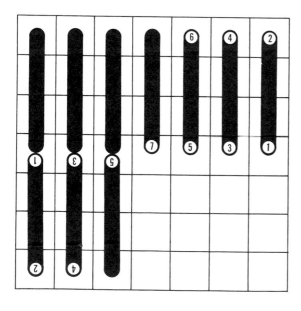

# GOBELIN OBLIQUE
### *(Slanting Gobelin)*

1¼ full strands = 1 sq. in.
1 color, shade or stripe
3-2-1 count
rotate canvas

Gobelin Oblique forms slanting ridges and a firm backing. It is excellent for use as a background or filler and gives a nice finished look when used to frame areas of other work.

The stitch is worked from right to left, rotating the canvas for each row. It is most successful when worked over a 3-2-1 count. Be careful to move over 2 mesh to the upper right or the slant will be lost. The first and last stitches of each row are compensating stitches over a 2-1-1 count.

Keep an easy tension, as this stitch tends to pull the canvas permanently out of shape, and avoid twisting the yarn while working. Backstitching between the rows is attractive.

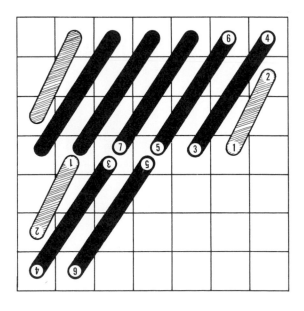

# 4
## SPLIT GOBELIN

1½ double strands = 1 sq. in.
1 color, shade
3-0-1 count
rotate canvas

This is a very attractive stitch that looks like tight knitting when worked up. It is useful for background, filler or detail, and it works up quickly. Split Gobelin has a firm backing.

The first row is worked exactly the same as a 3-0-1 count Gobelin Droit, except a double strand is used instead of a full strand. The successive rows still are worked over the 3-0-1 count, but they back up or encroach over 1 mesh of the previous row, splitting the yarn in half. After the first row, only 2 "new" mesh of canvas are used each time plus 1 of the "old."

Very subtle shading can be achieved by using closely related colors and by mixing one strand of each color together in intermediary rows.

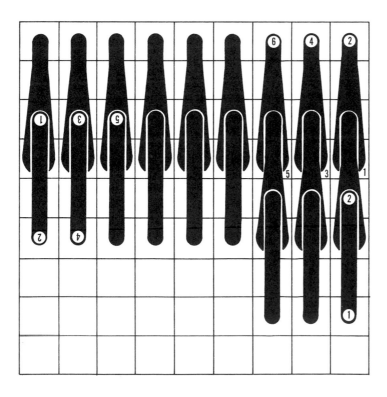

**5**

# INTERLOCKING GOBELIN
*(Encroaching Gobelin)*

1½ double strands = 1 sq. in.
1 or more colors, shade
3-0-1 count (up to 5-0-1)
rotate canvas

Interlocking Gobelin is basically the same as its counterpart, the Split Gobelin.
The difference is that here the back-up stitch fits to the side of the stitch in
the previous row, rather than splitting it in the middle.

Interlocking Gobelin can be worked over 2, 3, 4 or 5 horizontal mesh with
each successive row overlapping 1 mesh of the previous row. Be sure to be
consistent in going to the same side of the stitches when backing up into the
previous row.

Because the stitches fit in at the side of the previous stitches, they will
appear to be slanted. This stitch is good for backgrounds, and it forms a firm
backing. It is a long-wearing stitch.

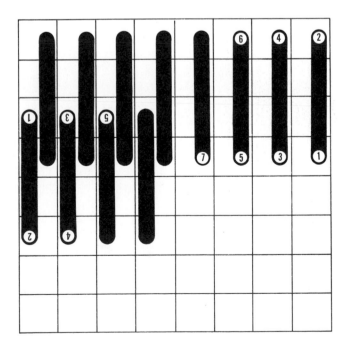

## 6
## OLD FLORENTINE

1 full strand = 1 sq. in.
1 or more colors
6-6, 2-2 or 9-9, 3-3 count
rotate canvas

Old Florentine consists of stitches worked in pairs over a count of 6, then 2. This count is consistent throughout; however, in each succeeding row long stitches meet short and short meet long. It is important to maintain an easy tension or canvas will show through at the tops and bottoms of the stitches. Old Florentine works up very quickly.

It is not recommended for upholstery or other articles that will receive extensive use, due to the length of the stitches and their susceptibility to snagging. It is attractive worked in dark colors, makes an excellent filler and lends itself very well to border motifs.

For variation, make the long stitches in one color and the short in a second color, or alternate colors with each row.

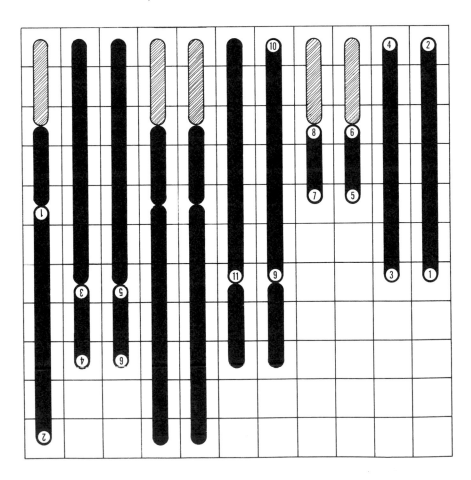

1½ full strands = 1 sq. in.
1 or 2 colors
2-0-2 or 4-0-2 count
rotate canvas

This stitch is similar to Gobelin Droit except there are 2 mesh between each stitch and 2 alternating rows of progress. The stitch can be worked over a 2-0-2 or 4-0-2 count with one or two colors. The stitch will not work over an odd number of mesh. If two colors are used, do all of one color first and then add the second color for a striped ribbon effect. Or do 2 rows of one color and then 2 rows of the second color.

The top and bottom rows will be missing stitches. To fill in, use a compensating stitch over a 1-0-2 or 2-0-2 count. This stitch works up quickly and has a firm backing. It makes an excellent background and can be used as a filler for such things as tree bark and flower petals.

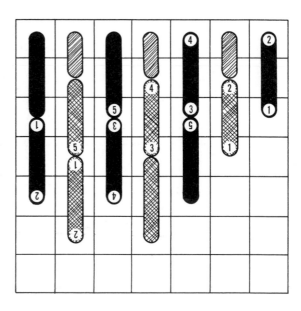

# 8
# PARISIAN

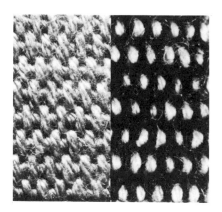

1½ full strands = 1 sq. in.
1 or more colors
4-0-2, 2-0-2 or 3-0-2, 1-0-2 count
rotate canvas

Parisian forms a pattern of interlocking long and short stitches, the long stitches of one row meeting the short in the adjacent rows and vice versa. A full strand of yarn is needed to adequately cover the canvas.

Parisian is excellent when worked in one or more colors. The second color can be introduced in alternate rows or as the short stitch; the effects are quite different. Whichever way you decide to work in the second color, be sure to finish out both long and short stitches of a row before rotating the canvas to begin the next row. Also, it is easiest to work the long stitches in a row before working the short stitches.

This stitch has a firm backing and makes a good background or filler.

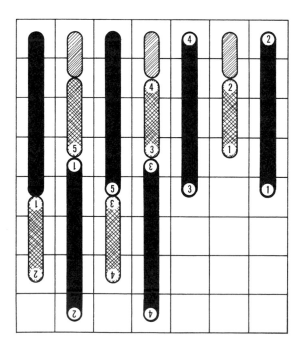

**9**

# HUNGARIAN
*(Point d'Hongrie)*

1¼ full strands = 1 sq. in.
1 or more colors
2-4-2 count
rotate canvas

Hungarian is a very simple stitch, consisting of 3 stitches with a 2-4-2 count, a space of 2 vertical mesh and then a repeat of the 2-4-2 pattern unit. Successive rows interlock with the long stitch fitting into the empty space and the short stitches meeting the short stitches of the preceding row.

Hungarian is firm and durable, has an excellent texture and works up quickly. It is excellent for use as a background in one color and looks nice in combination with other stitches.

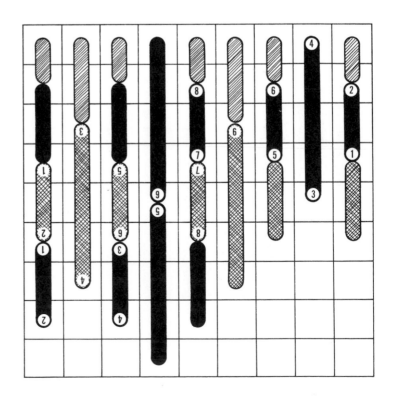

# 10

# HUNGARIAN GROUND

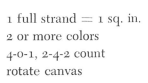

1 full strand = 1 sq. in.
2 or more colors
4-0-1, 2-4-2 count
rotate canvas

The first part of Hungarian Ground is a zigzag pattern of upright stitches covering 4 horizontal mesh. Spaces are created where Hungarian units fit in, again over a 2-4-2 count.

After completing a row of the second color, rotate the canvas and work the first color again over a 4-0-1 count. This row will be easier to count since you can use the Hungarian units as a guide in locating each new stitch of the zigzag operation. Note when doing the next row of Hungarian "diamonds" that their location will change slightly.

This is a highly decorative stitch that is particularly well suited to abstract or geometric designs. It has a firm backing and works up quickly.

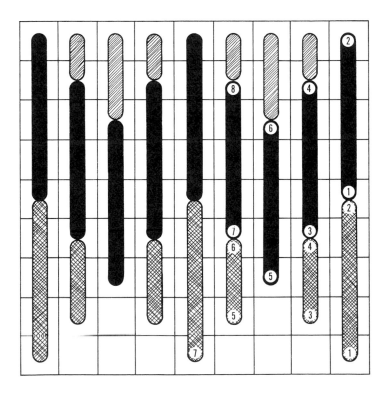

1½ double strands = 1 sq. in.
2 colors
4-4-4-4-1, 2-0-3 count
rotate canvas

The Shell stitch consists of 4 upright stitches drawn together in the middle by a horizontal tie-down stitch. The 4 upright stitches should not be pulled tight or the canvas will be pulled out of shape when they are tied down.

After completing all Shell units, introduce the second color by working a short 2-0-3 count stitch between each Shell. Or make small loops of the second color joining together the horizontal tie-downs as an attractive variation.

This is a strong texture stitch that looks particularly nice worked in rows or borders.

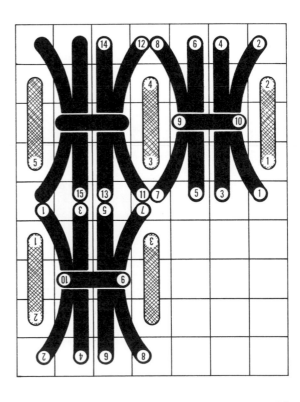

# 12
# FRENCH

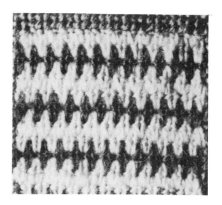

2¼ single strands = 1 sq. in.
1 or more colors
4-1-4-1-2 count
rotate canvas

French stitch is a double tie-down stitch. It works up very slowly but is worth the effort. Its finished appearance is quite delicate, and it is very tight and virtually snagproof.

At first it may seem that a single strand is not enough to adequately cover the canvas. However, as you work successive rows, you will see how the stitches interlock, forming a firm, well-covered surface.

French stitch is a good filler or background; however, you may want to confine its use to small areas since it takes so long to work up.

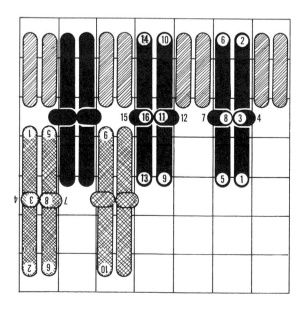

2 double strands = 1 sq. in.
1 color, shade
3-1 (alternate 5-1) count
rotate canvas

Knotted is a classical single tie-down stitch. Each successive row encroaches or backs up over 1 mesh of the previous row forming a firm, tight surface. The stitch works up quickly, and it is suitable as filler or a textured background.

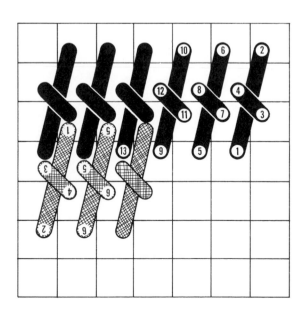

# 14
# ROCOCO

2¼ single strands = 1 sq. in
1 or more colors, shade
4-1 count
rotate canvas

Rococo is a fancy tie-down stitch that can be seen in many heritage samplers and other finished pieces. It is very slow to work up; however, its lacy appearance is well worth the effort.

The version of the Rococo shown here consists of 4 upright stitches that share the same hole at the top and bottom and which are individually tied down in place in the middle with 1 count horizontal stitches. Each row interlocks with the previous row.

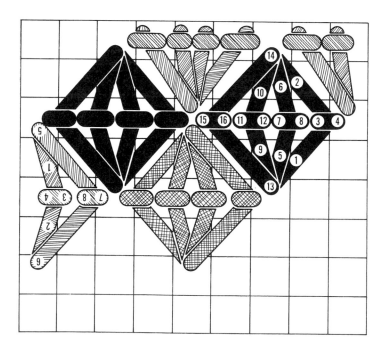

# 15
## STRAIGHT CROSS
### (Upright Cross)

2½ double strands = 1 sq. in.
1 or more colors, shade
2-2 count
rotate canvas

Straight Cross can be worked two ways. Traditionally, the cross is formed as a single unit, crossing 2 horizontal then 2 vertical mesh and then moving over 2 mesh to repeat the upright cross. However, if you are planning to cover a fairly large area, there is an easier, quicker method. First make all the upright stitches for a whole row. Then rotate the canvas and return, making the horizontal bar of each cross. It will seem less tedious to work the stitch this way.

Straight Cross is an excellent texture stitch and can be used for such things as tree bark, pavement and flower centers. In addition, it is a firm, snagproof stitch. A polka-dotted effect can be achieved by periodically substituting another color for one of the crosses.

Work with an even, easy tension and make sure all crosses are crossed in the same direction or sequence.

Method I

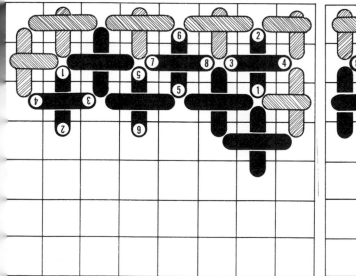

Method II

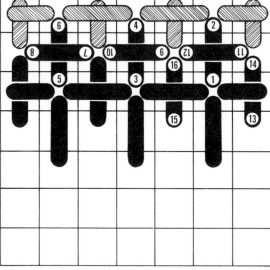

# 16
## CROSS

1¼ double strands = 1 sq. in.
1 color, shade
2-2 count
rotate canvas Method I only

Cross stitch is one of the oldest and most widely used embroidery stitches throughout history. Many ancient pieces have been found worked in this stitch alone.

Cross stitch is easy and quick to work up, and it is economical in wool use. There are two methods for working the stitch. It can be done as a single, complete unit going from bottom right to top left, then crossing bottom left to top right over 2 mesh each way. Or it can be done in two separate steps, making half of each unit across the row and completing the cross in each unit on the return trip. Make sure all units are crossed in the same direction.

The uses of Cross stitch are virtually limitless!

Method I

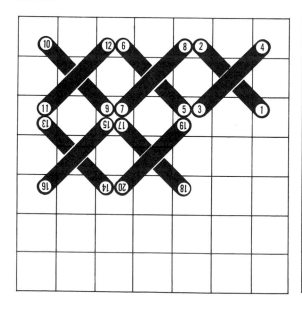

Method II

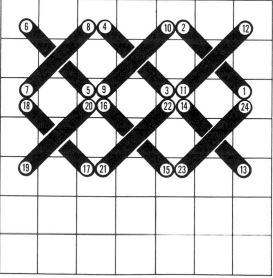

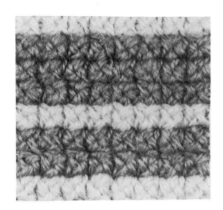

1½ double strands = 1 sq. in.
1 or more colors
3-3-3-3 (2-2-2-2) count
rotate canvas

Woven Cross can be worked as a regular canvas stitch or singly as an over-laid stitch. It is composed of identical 3 count crosses worked directly on top of each other. The last leg of the second cross is interwoven with the first leg of the first cross.

When worked up, it resembles tiny stars and is a highly decorative stitch worked in one or more colors.

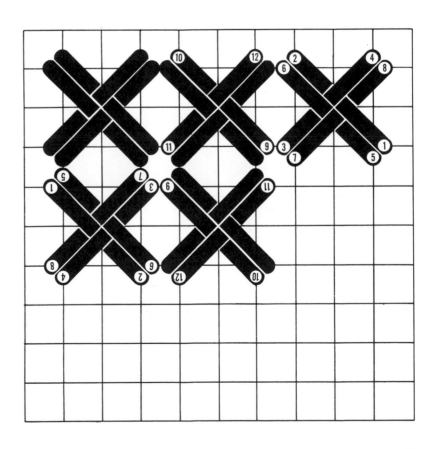

## 18

## OBLONG WITH BACKSTITCH

1 double or full strand = 1 sq. in.
1 color
4-4-2 count
rotate canvas

Oblong with Backstitch consists of a cross over a 4-2 count tied down in the middle with a 2 count Backstitch. This is an outstanding texture stitch and is shown off to best advantage in one color. It is especially good used in areas where a nubbly appearance is desired. In addition, it is firm and snag-resistant.

The use of a double or full strand will depend on the quality, color and thickness of the yarn you are using. Make a few trial stitches in the canvas margin before working this stitch in your project.

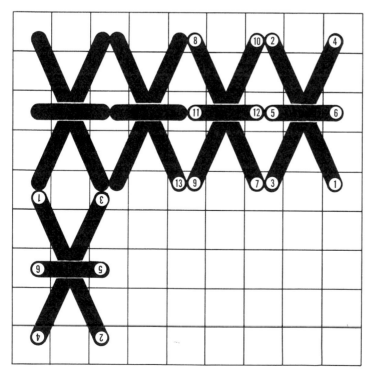

1 full strand = 1 sq. in.
1 or 2 colors
4-4-4-4 count
rotate canvas

Smyrna is composed of 2 units; first a large diagonal cross is worked, then an upright cross is worked on top. Be sure to cross the stitches in the same direction.

When working Smyrna in two colors, it is quicker to do all the diagonal crosses for a row and then all the upright crosses in the second color. Rotate the canvas and proceed as usual after a whole row is completed. When finished, Smyrna looks like a series of square tiles marked with crosses. This is a firm stitch that looks nice in borders or as background or filler.

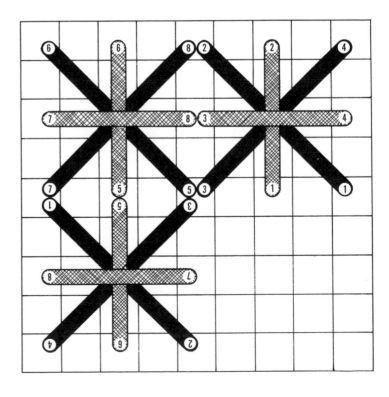

## 20

# LARGE CROSS–STRAIGHT CROSS

½ full strand = 1 sq. in. (diagonal cross)

¾ double strand = 1 sq. in. (upright cross)

1 or 2 colors

4-4-0, 2-2-4 count

rotate canvas

This is another 2-unit crossed stitch pattern. First the large diagonal crosses are worked, and then the smaller upright crosses are worked in between. Make sure each unit is crossed in the same direction.

The finished look of Large Cross–Straight Cross is very interesting—the small crosses look like French Knots peeping out from between the large crosses. This stitch works up quickly and is a good filler.

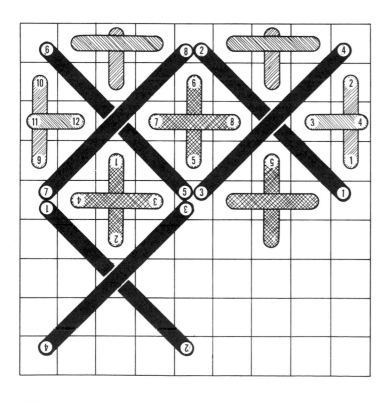

# CROSSED CORNERS
*(Rice, William and Mary)*

½ full strand = 1 sq. in (diagonal
  cross)
¾ double strand = 1 sq. in. (corner
  tie-downs)
4-4-0, 2-2-2-2 count
rotate canvas

Crossed Corners is a particularly beautiful stitch that sometimes resembles
tiny flowers when worked in two colors. It is a stitch that has been used in
canvas embroidery for decades and is often a part of heritage samplers.

The diagonal cross is worked first over a 4-4 count. Then each corner is
tied down diagonally with the second color over a 2-2 count. A double strand
of the second color is all that is needed to cover the canvas, and it gives the
tie-downs a delicate look. Once you get the feel of the stitching order of the
corner tie-downs, you will be able to swing your needle easily and move
along fairly quickly.

Crossed Corners is a strong, firm stitch that can be used as background,
filler or detail. It is attractive when worked with other stitches in a border.

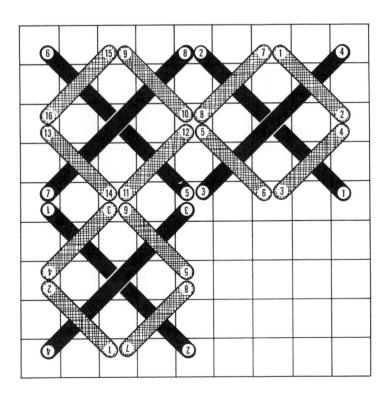

## 22
## DOUBLE STRAIGHT CROSS

1 color: 2 double or full strands =
   1 sq. in.
2 colors: 1 double or full strand =
   1 sq. in. (upright cross) ½ double
   strand = 1 sq. in. (diagonal cross)
1 or 2 colors
4-4, 2-2 count
rotate canvas

If you are using one color for Double Straight Cross, the entire unit will be made in one operation. First a 4-4 count upright cross is made, and then a diagonal 2-2 count cross is worked on top.

If working with two colors, make a complete row of upright crosses, then fill in with the diagonal crosses using the second color. Successive rows interlock. You probably will need to experiment to see whether a double or full strand will be adequate to cover the canvas.

Double Straight Cross is an outstanding texture stitch, the effect being somewhat like a series of tiny pyramids. This is a tight, firm stitch.

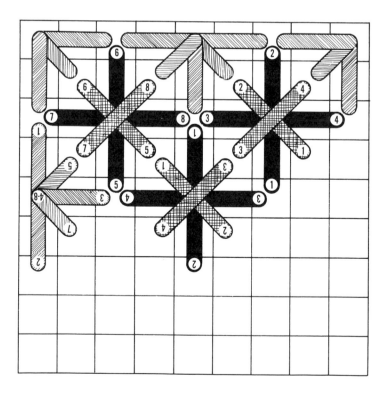

1 full strand = 1 sq. in.
1 or more colors
6-6-0, 2-2-0 count
rotate canvas

This pattern is composed of two different sized interlocking crosses. The large oblong cross is worked over a 6-2 count; the smaller diagonal cross is worked over a 2-2 count.

Double stitch can be troublesome at first if you aren't careful to observe the count. Notice in the diagram that each cross is begun directly above or below the one before it, skipping *no* vertical mesh. The second row interlocks, with the long cross meeting short, and vice versa. Be sure to cross all units in the same direction.

This stitch is one that is particularly striking when worked in one color. It works up quickly and can be used to great advantage as a background. Double stitch probably will become one of your favorites.

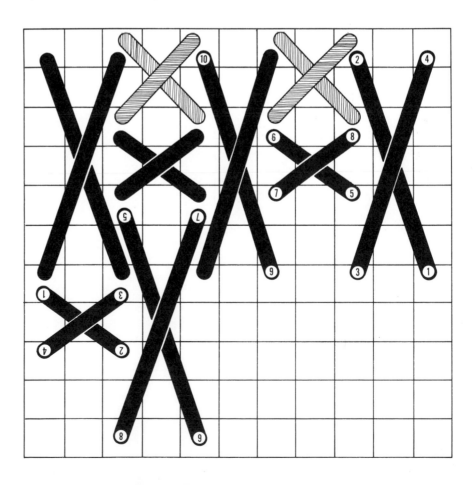

# 24
# ITALIAN CROSS

1½ double strands = 1 sq. in.
1 color
3-3-3-3 (or 2-2-2-2) count
rotate canvas

Italian Cross actually is a box with a diagonal cross inside. It is shown here starting at the right side of the canvas. However, if you prefer, you can start it just as well at the left side.

Start the unit by making the 3 count cross and then fill in the frame. This is a sturdy stitch that can be used for background or filler.

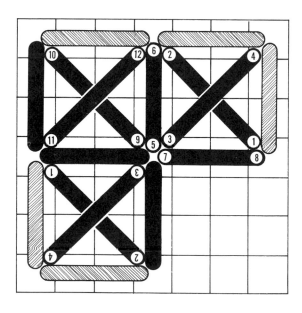

## 25
## LONG-ARMED CROSS
*(Greek, Long-Legged Cross, Double-Back)*

1¼ double strands = 1 sq. in.
1 color, stripe
2-2-2-4 count
rotate canvas

A version of Long-Armed Cross is used exclusively in the traditional Swedish canvas embroidery, Tvistsöm. Its finished appearance is a tightly interwoven braid; the surface is like a luxuriously stitched tapestry.

When working Long-Armed Cross, proceed up and ahead 2, back up 2, down and ahead 4, back up 2, up and ahead 2, back up 2, and so forth. To finish out a row, go down 1 mesh and to the right 2 mesh.

Rotate the canvas and return in the same manner, making sure the stitches of the new row are interlocking properly with those of the previous row. You will see ridges developing, and after several rows are completed, the characteristic pattern with ridges close together and then far apart will be formed. Long-Armed Cross makes an excellent border.

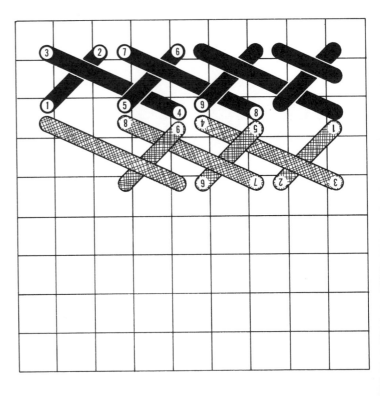

Wall hanging worked in Tvistsöm, from an old Swedish pattern. Mrs. Grant D. Ross, Denver.

73

## 26
## OBLIQUE SLAV

1 full strand = 1 sq. in.
1 color, stripe, shade
2-4-2 count
rotate canvas

Oblique Slav is another stitch that looks woven. The stitch is worked from left to right, rotating the canvas to begin each new row. The characteristic slant of the stitch is formed by going up over 2 mesh and ahead over 4 mesh. Compensate at the beginning and end of each row with a stitch crossing 1 horizontal and 2 vertical mesh.

Oblique Slav works up quickly and makes excellent stripes. It can be used as filler or background; however, it is not snagproof and should not be used for articles that will receive heavy wear.

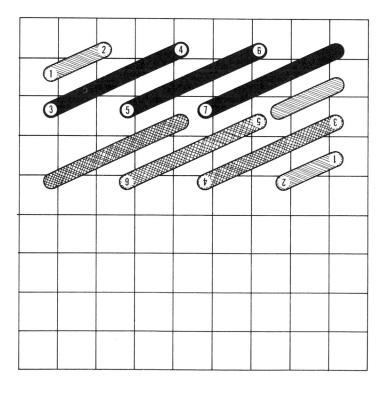

# ENCROACHING OBLIQUE

1½ full strands = 1 sq. in.
1 or more colors, shade
1-4-2 count
rotate canvas

Encroaching Oblique is worked in rows from left to right. Make each stitch by going ahead over 4 mesh and down over 1 mesh. Move back under 2 mesh and up under 1 mesh to find the starting hole for the next stitch.

Encroaching Oblique makes an excellent background or filler and is quick to work up. It can be worked in stripes or in shaded areas.

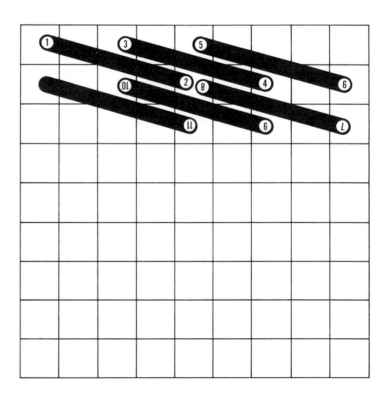

## 28
## HERRINGBONE
*(Plaited Gobelin)*

1¼ full strands = 1 sq. in.
1 or more colors, shade
4-2 count
do not rotate canvas

Herringbone gets its name from the woven, tweedy effect it produces. Unlike the procedure with many other stitches, all rows must be started at the left side of the area to be covered, and the canvas must not be rotated for alternate rows or the pattern will be lost.

Herringbone progresses ahead 4 mesh either up or down and then backs up 2 mesh. To secure the beginning of each new row, you can weave along under the stitching on the reverse side of the canvas back to the starting point. Or hold a long tail of yarn against the reverse side, tying it down with the first several stitches of the new row. Each row is ended in the normal way.

Another hint to keep the rhythm and ease of stitching is to have the yarn above your hand when proceeding down and below your hand when proceeding up. This holds true for all Herringbone stitches. Be consistent in the direction of crossing each unit.

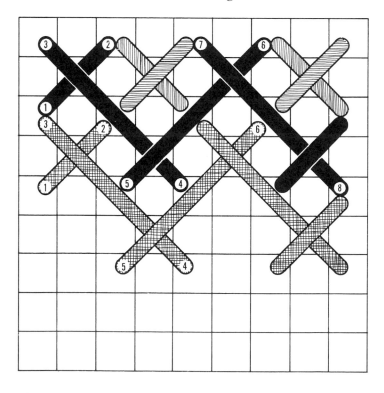

# HERRINGBONE GONE WRONG

1½ full strands = 1 sq. in.
1 color
4-2 count
rotate canvas

The first row of Herringbone Gone Wrong is worked the same way as Herringbone. Then, the "no-rotating" rule for Herringbones is broken in the second row. To work this stitch, continue to rotate the canvas and diagram for each successive row. If you look closely, you will see that each stitch falls either directly 2 above or 2 below the stitch of the previous row.

Herringbone Gone Wrong is an excellent texture stitch and works well as background or filler.

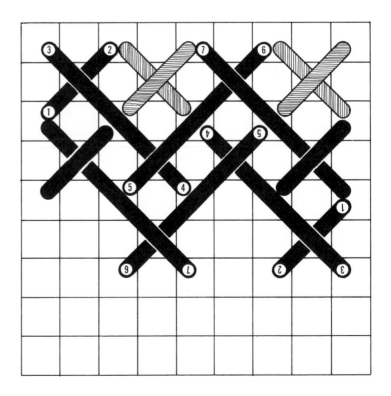

## 30

# INTERWOVEN HERRINGBONE
*(Bazaar)*

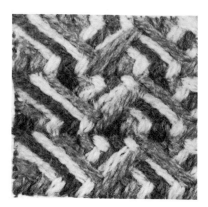

1 double or full strand = 1 sq. in.
4 to 6 colors
8-2 count
do not rotate canvas

Interwoven Herringbone is simply a "6 trip" Herringbone. The first row
starts 6 mesh from the top with a compensating stitch worked down and to
the right 2 with a back up over 2. From there, you move up to the right 8,
back up 2, down ahead to the right 8, and back up 2. The row is ended by
going down 6 from the last back-up stitch at the top.

The canvas must not be rotated for this stitch. The second color will begin
2 mesh above the hole where the first color began and will start off with a
4-2 compensating stitch. From then on the 8-2 count is followed. All successive rows will alternate in location 2 above or to the right of the previous
row. The lettered circles in the diagram indicate the starting points.

Interwoven Herringbone is one of the most dramatic canvas stitches. It
looks beautiful when several shades of one color are used and equally as
beautiful when contrasting colors are used. The pattern it creates is striking
enough in itself to use for covering whole pieces, and it is an effective border.

The stitch can also be worked over a 4-1 count. Experiment with a double
or full strand before working an area of the stitch.

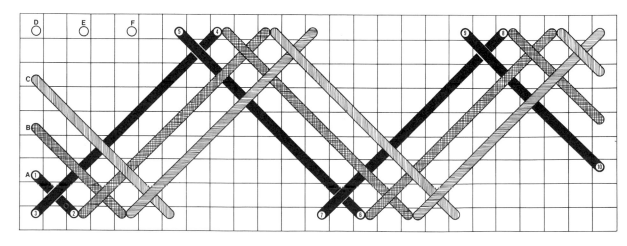

# COUCHING STITCHES

## HERRINGBONE COUCHING

1 full strand = 1 sq. in. (first color)
½ double strand = 1 sq. in. (second color)
4-0-1, 4-2 count
rotate canvas for first color only

A single row of Herringbone can be used very effectively to couch down another kind of stitch. Here, a Gobelin Droit over a 4 count is shown couched with a Herringbone stitch over a 4-2 count. Each Herringbone row starts and ends with a 2-2 compensating stitch.

Herringbone Couching is especially attractive when worked in a contrasting color to the understitching. It creates a festive look and makes an excellent border. You might consider using metal thread for the couching stitch.

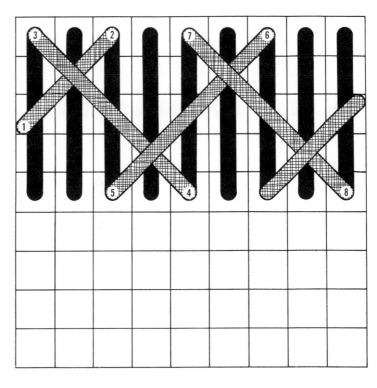

## 32
# BOKHARA COUCHING
*(Bamboo)*

1¼ double or full strands = 1 sq. in.
1 or 2 colors
any count
do not rotate canvas

Bokhara Couching is a long stitch running from left to right over any number of vertical mesh. It is couched or tied down on the return with short upright stitches over a 1 count. These tie-down stitches will look quite different depending on whether even or uneven spacing within the row is used. Another factor in the finished look is the location of the tie-down stitches in relation to tie-downs in surrounding rows.

Couch each row as you go along and do not leave too long a distance without couching, for the yarn may snag easily. This is a special-effects stitch that resembles bamboo.

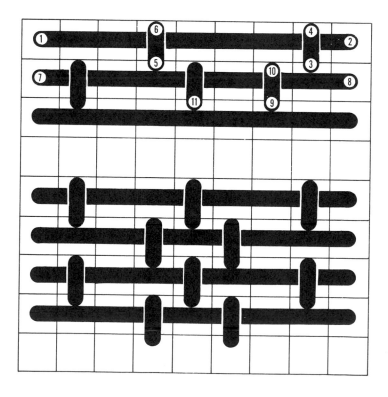

# ROUMANIAN COUCHING

1 double or full strand = 1 sq. in.
1 color
any count
do not rotate canvas

Roumanian Couching is underlaid with a stitch crossing any number of vertical mesh. Each long stitch is then tied down with diagonal stitches that cross 3 vertical and 1 horizontal mesh on the return. The stitch should be worked one row at a time, and there is no need to rotate the canvas for ease in stitching. The tie-downs can be evenly or unevenly spaced to create a particular pattern.

Experiment to see whether you will need a double or full strand for good canvas coverage. Roumanian Couching is another special-effects stitch that should not be used on articles that will receive hard wear due to the stitch's susceptibility to snagging.

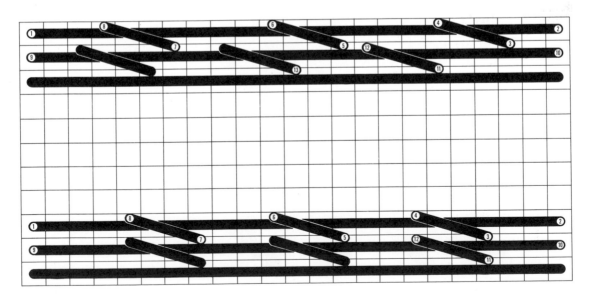

½ full strand = 1 sq. in. (long stitch)
1 double strand = 1 sq. in. (couching
  stitches)
1 or more colors
1-1-2 half cross, 1, 3, 5, etc. count
  (weaving stitch)
rotate canvas

Web closely resembles Bokhara Couching and tramé work, the finished result having a woven appearance. The least tedious way to perform this stitch is to make all the tie-down stitches first. These are nothing more than 1 count Tent stitches done in horizontal rows with 2 mesh between each stitch and each row.

After completing the tie-downs, begin the long stitches with the second color, weaving under each of the tie-downs diagonally with 2 mesh between each row.

An interesting effect can be created by changing colors partway through on the second step. Tent stitches can be added around the perimeter for finishing off the area. Do not stitch with a tight tension when making the tie-down stitches or it will be difficult to weave the long stitches underneath.

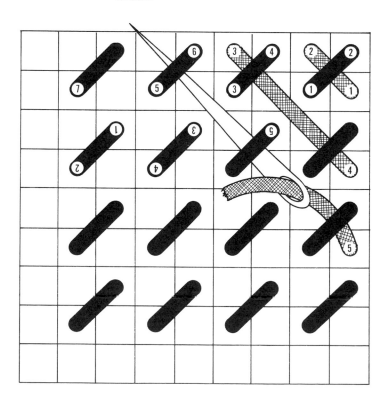

**35**

**STEM**

*(Long Oblique)*

1½ double strands = 1 sq. in.
2 double strands = 1 sq. in. if
    Backstitched
1 or more colors, stripe
rotate canvas

It is most comfortable to begin Stem, as well as other vertically worked stitches, at the left side of the area to be covered; however, it can be started at the right. Stem actually is a Gobelin Oblique worked vertically with each row changing its direction. Backstitches between each row or every other row are particularly effective with Stem.

This stitch is quick to work up and is excellent for use as a filler and for special effects such as grass and leaves.

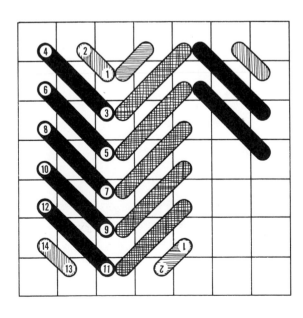

## 36
## FERN

1¼ double strands = 1 sq. in.
1 or more colors
3-4-2-3-4 count
do not rotate canvas

Fern is worked in vertical rows. Beginning in the upper left corner, go down 4 and to the right 3 mesh. Next, back up 2, go up 4 and to the right 3 to complete each unit. You will notice that each stitch is 4 mesh wide at the top and 2 mesh wide at the bottom. To form the next unit, move 2 mesh below where the first unit began and repeat the operation.

A 2 count cross compensating stitch is needed to fill in the top of the design. At the bottom cross each side of the last unit into the center hole. Do not try to rotate the canvas when working Fern. When finished, Fern resembles corduroy or a vertical braid. It looks very nice Backstitched between the rows.

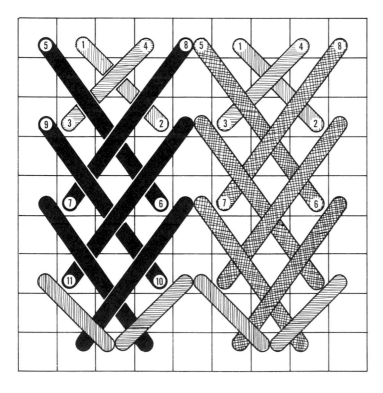

1½ double strands = 1 sq. in.
1 or more colors
3-2-2, 3-2-2 count
rotate canvas

Vandyke is worked in vertical rows forming a unique braided pattern. Each stitch unit is composed of 2 sections each crossing 3 horizontal and 2 vertical mesh. All new units encroach 1 mesh into the previous unit. This stitch is quick to work up and can be used effectively in narrow areas.

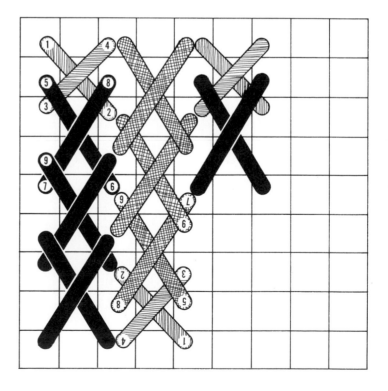

**38**

# FISHBONE
*(Long and Short Oblique)*

1 full strand = 1 sq. in.
1 or more colors
4-1-2 count
rotate canvas

Each unit is made up of a diagonal stitch that slants up and to the right 4 mesh (except for the first compensating stitch). This stitch then is tied in place with a small reverse Tent stitch over a 1 count. The first stitch of each row will cover only 2 vertical and 2 horizontal mesh and then is tied down with the usual Tent stitch. A 2 count cross is needed to compensate at the end of the rows.

An interesting zigzag effect can be created by alternating the direction of the rows. Fishbone is a popular stitch that is useful for background or filler.

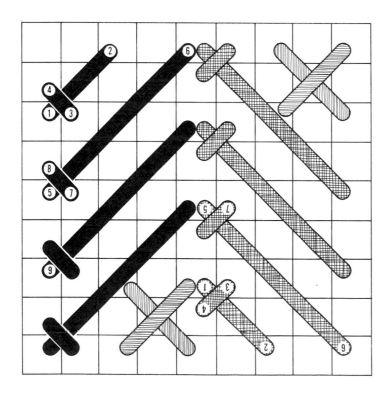

Jerusalem by Mrs. Ben Marcus of Milwaukee is a striking example of how richly textured a needlepoint piece can be when several stitches are used in combination. The Split Gobelin sky has been delicately shaded, and the pink Jacquard mountains below present a good contrast. Many stitches have been used in the buildings, including Old Florentine, Tent, Flat, Parisian, Crossed Corners and Bokhara Couching. The stone wall at the bottom is worked in Brick over a 2 and 4 count. Designed by Subo.

This kneeling cushion for the Tabor Academy chapel communion rail was worked by Mrs. Frank B. Jewett, Jr., of New Canaan, Conn., and designed by Mili Holmes. Note the movement and rhythm of the design created by gracefully curved and swirling lines.

Henri Gadbois, a prominent Houston artist, became interested in needlepoint. These lovely floral pillows are his designs. Mr. Gadbois, his wife, and several friends did the stitching, and the pillows were ready for a gala opening of a show of his paintings.

The Coexistence Tree was worked by Mrs. James P. Caffrey of Wakefield, R.I., and designed by Mili Holmes. The vibrant colors were created by mixing strands of closely related colors together and stitching with them simultaneously. Diagonal Mosaic and Mosaic are used in addition to Tent. The cats' whiskers have been overstitched.

2 double strands = 1 sq. in.
1 or more colors
2 count
rotate canvas

Chain stitch is very similar to Knitting stitch. It usually is worked vertically. Chain also can be worked diagonally or around curves as an overlaid stitch, making it excellent for outlining, initialing, and so forth.

Each loop stitch ties down the loop preceding it. You can work over any number of mesh, depending on where the stitch is being used and the effect you wish to create. It is shown here over a 2 count.

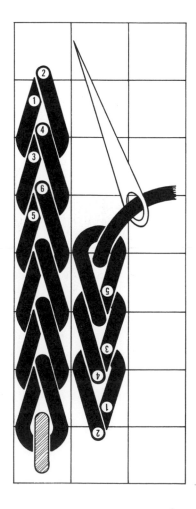

## 40
## KNITTING
*(Kalem)*

1½ double strands = 1 sq. in.
1 or more colors, shade
4-1-2 count
do not rotate canvas

Knitting stitch is worked in vertical rows. Unlike most other vertically worked stitches which begin in the upper left, Knitting is begun in the lower right corner. Each stitch covers 4 horizontal and 1 vertical mesh with 2 mesh between each stitch. The top and bottom should be compensated with a 2-1 count stitch. When ascending, you work from the center up and out. When descending, you work from the outside down into the center.

Knitting stitch creates a tight, durable surface which is good for filler.

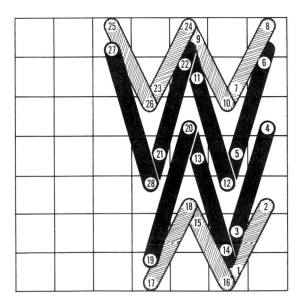

# DIAGONAL STITCHES WORKED FROM
# UPPER LEFT TO LOWER RIGHT

1½ double strands = 1 sq. in.
2 colors
1-2-1 count
rotate canvas

Mosaic is started at the upper left corner and is worked diagonally to the lower right corner. It is composed of 3 stitches. The first crosses 1 horizontal and 1 vertical mesh, the second crosses 2 horizontal and 2 vertical mesh, and the third crosses 1 horizontal and 1 vertical mesh (as in the first). The long stitches of each row touch the long stitches of the adjacent rows. Upon completing each 3 stitch unit, swing the needle straight down 2 mesh to the starting hole of the new unit.

This stitch is firmly backed, and when worked in two colors, forms a checkerboard pattern. Pay special attention to the tension of your stitching. Diagonally worked stitches tend to pull the canvas out of shape when the tension is too tight. Also, the yarn has a tendency to twist while working, which can make the stitches look thin. Let the needle dangle from the canvas to unwind the thread periodically while working diagonal stitches.

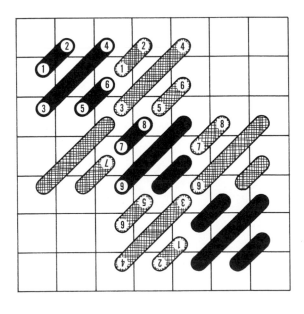

1½ double strands = 1 sq. in.
2 colors
1-2-3-2-1 count
rotate canvas

Flat stitch is worked diagonally. The 5-stitch units form squares, the long stitches of one color touching the long stitches of the same color in the adjacent rows. On completing a unit, swing the needle straight down 2 mesh to locate the correct starting hole for each new unit.

After completing all units of the first color, rotate the canvas 90°, and with the second color, repeat the same pattern units, rotating completely at the bottom of each row.

The use of two colors with the stitch units slanting in two directions produces a quilted effect. Some very attractive variations can be produced by rearranging the colors. For instance, you can make the first and last stitches of each unit in both directions a different color from the rest of the stitches, creating a series of relief boxes.

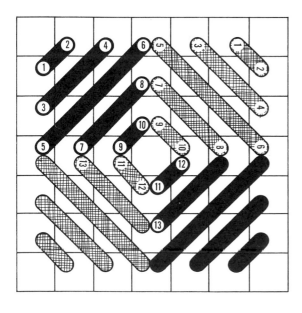

1¾ double strands = 1 sq. in.
2 colors
1-2-1 count
rotate canvas

Small Chequer actually is a combination of Mosaic and Tent. First make all Mosaic units in one color, moving over 2 mesh and down 1 mesh to the right or down 3 mesh to the left when you rotate the canvas to start a new row. Then work 4 Tent stitches between each Mosaic unit in another color. The long stitches of the Mosaic units should touch the long stitches in adjacent rows.

This stitch makes a very firm, durable surface and looks attractive as a background.

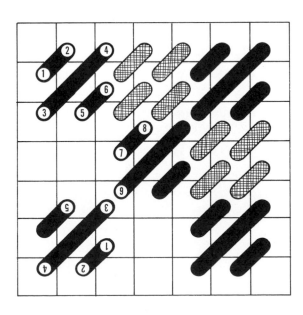

**44**

## LARGE CHEQUER

1½ double strands = 1 sq. in.
2 colors
1-2-3-2-1 count
rotate canvas

Large Chequer is a variation of the Flat stitch. First work all Flat units in one color. When completing a row, move over 3 mesh and down 1 mesh to return at the right or move straight down 4 mesh to return at the left. Then work 9 Tent stitches between each Flat unit in the second color. This is another good background stitch. Also, it looks nice in borders.

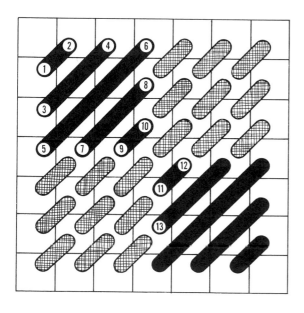

1½ double strands = 1 sq. in.
2 or more colors
1-2-3-2 count
do not rotate canvas

The first color of this stitch is worked like Flat, but there is no skipping between units. The 1-2-3-2 pattern is repeated without interruption all the way down from upper left corner to lower right corner. Then, this is framed on either side by Tent stitches worked down one side and up the other in another color.

Do not try to rotate the canvas when beginning the second row of the first color, as it is difficult to follow the count. There will be a 1-1 compensating stitch at the start of the usual pattern whether returning to the right or the left. Alternate between the first pattern and the Tent stitches as you work.

This stitch is an attractive background. Make sure that you are not stitching with too tight a tension, especially when working the stitch over a large area.

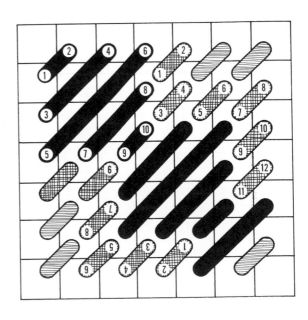

## 46
## BYZANTINE

1½ double strands = 1 sq. in.
2 or more colors, shade
2-2-2-2-2 count
(optional 3 count)
do not rotate canvas

Byzantine is a striking stitch whether worked in various bold colors or shaded. Except for the first compensating stitch, it progresses with a 2-2-1 count in units of 5 horizontal then 5 vertical stitch groups, forming a zigzag pattern from upper left to lower right corner. Start each successive row to the right or left, first making a 1-count compensating stitch and then proceeding with the usual 2-2-1 pattern.

You can vary the zigzag width by adding or subtracting stitches to the usual groupings of 5. Byzantine is an excellent filler and makes a beautiful border motif.

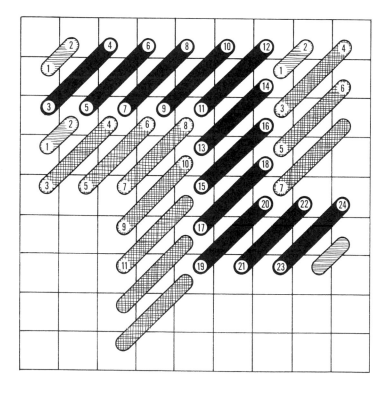

1½ double strands = 1 sq. in.
1 or more colors, shade, stripe
1-2 count
rotate canvas

Diagonal Mosaic forms a bold, "saw-toothed" diagonal stripe. The pattern is worked with an uninterrupted 1-2 count from upper left to lower right. It works up quickly, has a firm backing and probably is one of the most popular diagonal stitches.

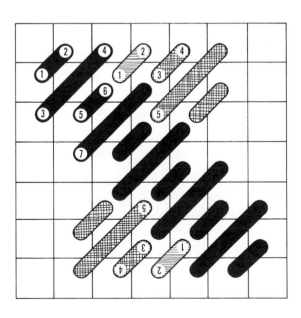

## 48
## DIAGONAL SCOTCH

1½ double strands = 1 sq. in.
2 or more colors, shade
2-3-4-3 count
rotate canvas

Diagonal Scotch follows a 2-3-4-3 count without any skipping between stitch units. After completing the first row, make a 1-2-2 compensating stitch on each of the following rows.

Diagonal Scotch forms a bold diagonal stripe pattern. It works up quickly and forms a firm backing. It can be used as background or filler. Its striking pattern can stand alone in projects such as eyeglass cases, luggage rack straps or pillows.

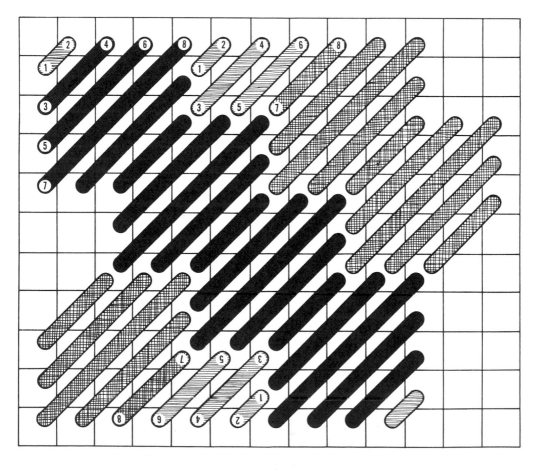

1½ double strands = 1 sq. in.
2 or more colors
1-2-2-1 count
rotate canvas

The Cashmere worked in two colors looks like Mosaic except that it forms rectangles instead of squares. Each unit is comprised of 4 diagonal stitches over a count of 1-2-2-1. Move down 2 horizontal mesh between each unit to the beginning of the next.

This stitch has a tendency to pull the canvas out of shape, so stitch with an easy tension. Cashmere is excellent for backgrounds and filler.

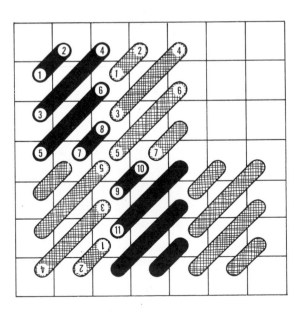

## 50
## DIAGONAL CASHMERE

1½ double strands = 1 sq. in.
2 or more colors
1-2-2 count
rotate canvas

Diagonal Cashmere is a tight stitch that can be used for background or filler. It is similar to Diagonal Mosaic, forming a continuous pattern of 1-2-2 units from upper left to lower right corners. Be careful to work with an easy tension.

Diagonal Cashmere works up quickly and forms a striking pattern that can stand alone in a project. If you are having trouble with the stitch count, do not rotate the canvas.

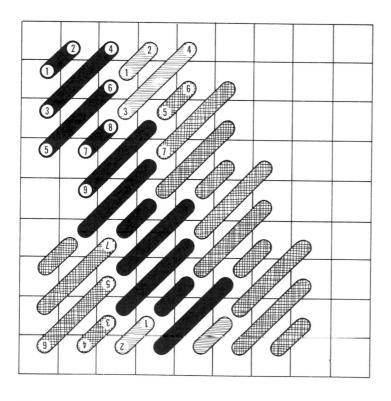

1½ double strands = 1 sq. in.
2 or more colors
2-2-2-2-2 count
rotate canvas

Jacquard is composed of two different stitches, the Byzantine and Tent. After making a compensating stitch over a 1 count, begin the 2-2-2-2-2 pattern. Upon completion of 1 row of the first color, frame both sides of the diagonal zigzag with Tent stitches in the second color. Alternate between these two patterns and colors.

Jacquard works up quickly and can be used as a filler or background.

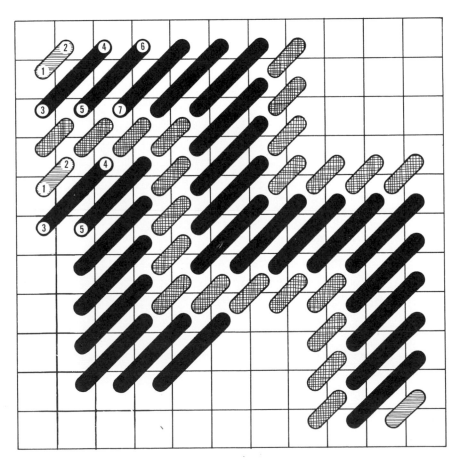

## 52
## MILANESE

1¼ double strands = 1 sq. in.
2 or more colors
1-2-3-4 count
rotate canvas

Milanese is a striking stitch with a unique pattern, its direction reversing with each row. It is worked over a 1-2-3-4 count from upper left to lower right corner. To start each new stitch unit, move over to the right 2 mesh and up 1 mesh and begin the 1-2-3-4 count again.

When returning, the short 1 count stitch of 1 row will share a hole with the longest stitches of the adjacent rows. Milanese makes an exotic background or filler. Again, be careful to stitch with an easy tension.

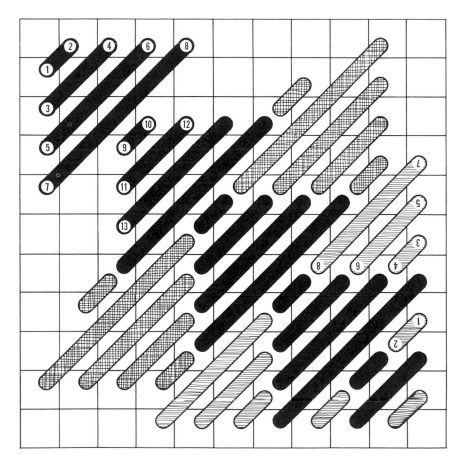

## FLORENTINE STITCHES

There is a whole family of canvas stitches that reached a high level of development in the late 1500s and has since continued to flourish. This family is called variously Hungarian Point (*Point d'Hongrie*), flame (*fiamma*), Bargello and Florentine.

There is an abundance of legend surrounding this family of stitches, which undoubtedly has given rise to the number of names associated with it. One of the most popular stories tells of a medieval Hungarian princess marrying into the powerful Medici family and bringing with her to Florence a trousseau embroidered with strange and exotic stitching. The name Bargello has been popularized by a contemporary writer who places the origins of these stitches in the Bargello, now the great museum in Florence. The name "flame" (*fiamma* in Italian) describes the look of one typical pattern in the family. Most scholars in the field, however, refer to this family of canvas stitches as Florentine work, which is, historically, a more accurate and comprehensive designation.

Florentine work is easily distingushed from other kinds of canvas embroidery as the stitches, which always are vertical or horizontal, characteristically are worked in various repeat patterns of steps and blocks. In addition to the famous flame patterns, many stylized floral motifs, chevrons, zigzags and other designs were developed. These have been used extensively to embellish both ecclesiastical pieces and domestic articles. Florentine work has been particularly popular for upholstery.

Easy chair with original Florentine stitch cover in a stylized carnation pattern. Worked between 1760 and 1780 in Massachusetts. *Courtesy of Bayou Bend Collection, The Museum of Fine Arts, Houston.*

Small pouch worked in wool on linen. American, 18th century. Note the accidental pattern changes due to miscounting. *Courtesy of the Cooper-Hewitt Museum of Design, Smithsonian Institution, New York.*

Modern adaptation of the carnation theme by Mary Conrad White, Gates Mills, Ohio.

Detail of Mrs. White's Florentine carnation pattern.

Traditionally, Florentine patterns were in two or three color groups with several intermediary shades in each group. While this effect can be used to great advantage in contemporary pieces, it is not necessary to stay within these boundaries when planning a design. If you do plan to shade the piece, it is suggested that you number the colors you are using to avoid confusion while working with the closely related shades.

The most important thing is to set up the first row very carefully, counting each stitch and double checking to make sure it is correct. After this, each row will fall into place, and the work will go very quickly.

The next seven stitches are modern adaptations of the basic Florentine work idea. You will notice that some of the stitches are horizontal and some are vertical, but still there are no crossed stitches in the group. The concept of repeat geometrics has been retained. The diagram numbers have been omitted, since these patterns can be worked in the order you find most comfortable. Also, the striped screen here represents a third color rather than a compensating stitch.

Note that Hungarian (No. 9) and Hungarian Ground (No. 10) both are Florentine patterns. However, they are used so extensively in needlepoint that they have been placed in the regular canvas stitch group.

Florentine stitch necktie by Betty Robison, Sand Lake, New York.

A happy frog with Florentine tummy by Pat Sampson, Houston.

# 53
## DIAMONDS

1½ double strands = 1 sq. in.
4 to 6 colors
4-0-2 count
rotate canvas

The basic pattern in this Florentine design covers 4 horizontal mesh and moves either up or down 2 mesh with each position change. After establishing 3 rows of different colors, turn the canvas upside down and work 3 more rows. This procedure will form the diamonds which can be filled in at the center with 4 count stitches of still another color.

Diamonds works up extremely well in bold, contrasting colors and is reminiscent of Indian beadwork patterns.

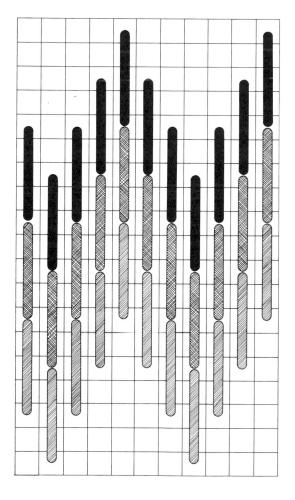

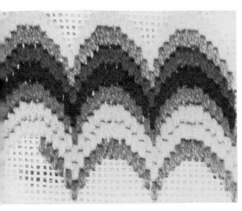

1 full strand = 4½ Scallops
shade, stripe
3 count or longer
rotate canvas

This very simple Florentine pattern is set up here over a 3 count and is worked most easily from right to left. If you are planning to have the Scallops all go in the same direction, you can start the first row at the upper right section of the canvas.

An interesting variation is to work 3 or 4 rows of Scallops and then turn the canvas upside down and work 3 or 4 rows in the other direction. Oval shapes will result where the rows touch, and these can be filled in with another canvas stitch or small design motif. The "cameos" should fall in the center of the canvas, and you will have to account for this when counting out and establishing the first rows.

Worked upside down on small canvas, the Scallop pattern makes effective ocean waves. Another variation can be produced by working the stitches over a 4 or 5 count.

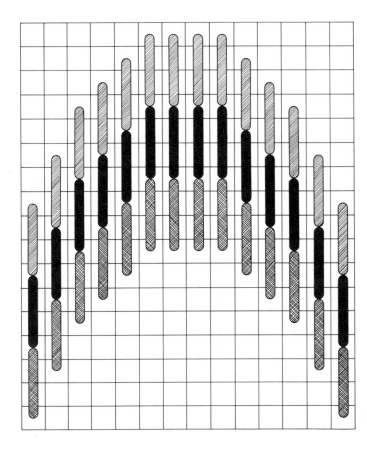

## 55
# DOUBLE WEAVE

1 full strand = 1¾ sq. in. (first 2 colors)
1 full strand = 3 sq. in. (third color)
3 colors
5-5 count
rotate canvas

This pattern is set up in two steps. Start the first color in the lower right corner and make pairs of vertical stitches over a 5 count, working diagonally to the upper left. Then, rotating the canvas at the end of each row, fill in the rest of the first color units. Turn the canvas sideways and repeat the above procedure with the second color. You will notice that there are little blocks of bare canvas showing through between the vertical and horizontal stitch units.

Now the fun begins! To fill in the spaces, secure a strand of the third color and bring it through to the front in the lower right corner. Weave it under the ends of the horizontal threads, but stay on the surface of the canvas. Rotate at the end of each row and fill in all the spaces in this direction. Then turn the canvas sideways and start weaving again at the lower right corner, going under the ends of the horizontal stitch units and over the first weaving threads.

When you are finished, it will appear that you have woven on the straight grain and the diagonal grain of the canvas to form a kind of latticework. You can do large areas of this pattern in minutes. Work with an easy tension for both steps. (Compensating stitches have been shown in this diagram.)

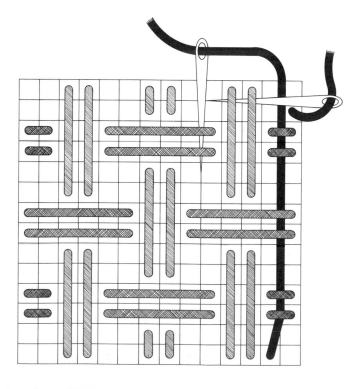

# CHRISTMAS TREES

1 full strand = 6 "branches"
2 or more colors
1-2-3-4-5 or 5-4-3-2-1 count
rotate canvas

Christmas Trees is a pattern made of regularly stacked interlocking triangles. The easiest way to set up this pattern is to work each group of triangles in vertical rows. If worked in two colors, the upright trees should be dark and the upside down trees should be light. Use more colors to create perspective.

This pattern is particularly well suited to pieces made in strips, such as suspenders and glasses cases. If viewed sideways, the Christmas Trees become arrows.

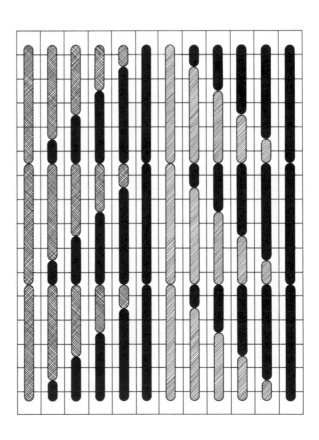

## 57

## RICKRACK

1 full strand = 3 zigzags
1 full strand = 6 diamonds
3 or more colors
4-0-1 (zigzag), 2-4-2 small (diamond),
   2-4-6-8-6-4-2 (large diamond)
rotate canvas

This Florentine pattern is worked in superimposed zigzag rows with intervening large and small diamonds. The zigzag rows alternate in being "on top" or "underneath."

The easiest way to set up this pattern is to work an "on top" zigzag row over a 4 count with 1 mesh between each stitch in groups of 8 stitches. Then fill in an "underneath" zigzag row. The diamonds can be filled in after that, working from right to left.

There are many color variations you can employ to change the look of the pattern. You could use the first color for all "on top" zigzags, the second color for all "underneath" zigzags and the third color for the diamonds. Or, as illustrated here, you can alternate the first and second colors for "on top" and "underneath" rows.

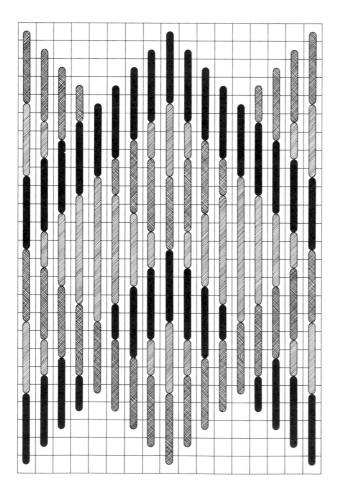

108

1 full strand = 2½ sq. in.
2 colors
6-0-1 count
rotate canvas

Op Boxes are a pattern created by opposing color areas of Gobelin Droit. This is set up from the middle out. First make 2 blocks of the first color, 6 stitches in each block over a 6 count. These blocks will be in upper right and lower left center positions. Then fill in the lower right and upper left center blocks with the second color. From now on as you work outward, the succeeding rows of blocks will create frames for the inner blocks with "negative" and "positive" colors touching.

You can continue all the way to the edge of the piece with bigger and bigger frames, or you can make a series of smaller Op Boxes to cover the piece. Keep the tension easy as you stitch as there is a tendency for canvas to show through between the rows.

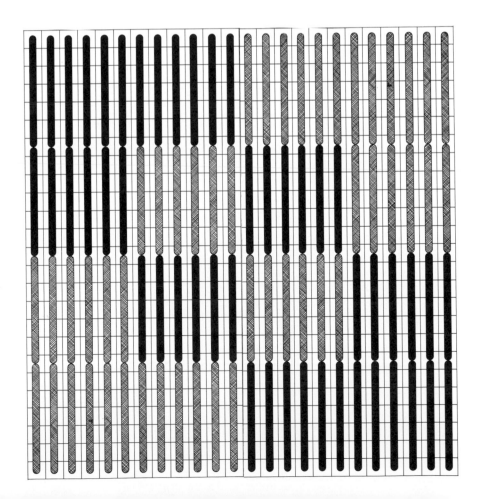

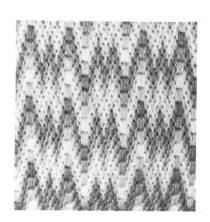

1 full strand = 1 large "W"
4 or more colors, shade
6 count
do not rotate canvas

This pattern follows the tradition of the classical Florentine designs and probably is most effective set up in two or more shades of different color families. Start at the upper right section of the canvas and establish the first row from right to left, counting very carefully. The stitches are worked over a 6 count, moving up or down 4 mesh to the next starting hole.

To make the peaks and valleys narrower or wider, add or subtract stitches to the groups of 3.

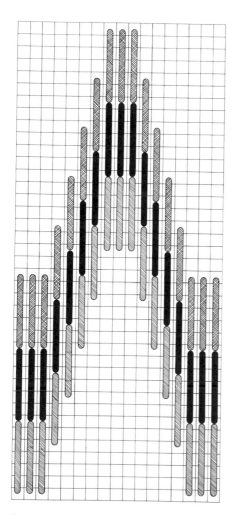

# SPECIAL STITCHES

2 double strands = 1 sq. in.
1 or more colors
2 count
rotate canvas

Begin the Star stitch in the lower right corner of your work. It is easiest to work each leg of the star clockwise, *always* going from the outside down into the center (E on the diagram). Rotate the canvas 90° with the completion of each quarter. Later, a short filler stitch can be worked between the legs. Each new Star will begin out of the same hole as the top or side of the previous one. The canvas can be rotated for new rows.

This highly decorative stitch can be used as filler or as a border motif.

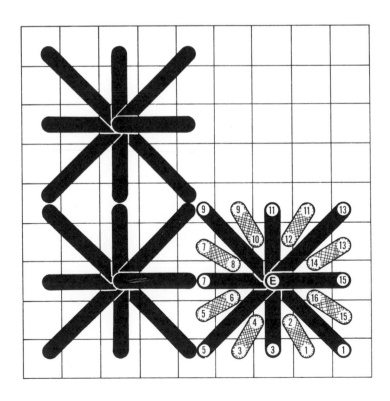

## 61
# DIAMOND EYELET

1½ double strands = 1 sq. in.
1 or more colors, shade
4-3-2-3 count
rotate canvas

Diamond Eyelet is a striking stitch that works up easily and quickly. Every spoke forming the Diamond is begun on the outside and always goes down into the center (E on the diagram). To find the starting hole for each new stitch, move directly to the left and up 1 mesh from the previous stitch. Work the stitch clockwise in quarters, rotating the canvas 90° for each quarter. Begin in the lower right corner. Each Diamond begins out of the top or side of the previous one. Compensate at the sides with a half or quarter of a Diamond. Work with an easy tension.

French Knots are an attractive addition to the centers of the Diamond Eyelet units.

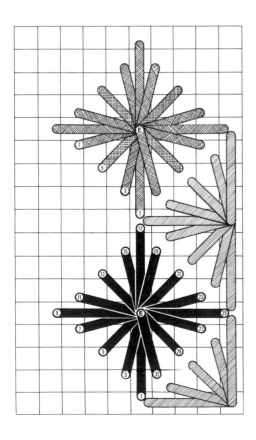

# TURKEY TUFTING
## (Surrey)

2 full strands = 1 sq. in.
1 color, shade
1-2-1-2 count
do not rotate canvas

Turkey Tufting is a classical stitch composed of tied-down loops that are cut to form a pile. When finished, the stitch produces a fuzzy surface and is worked somewhat like rug-hooking. The size of the loops will determine the depth of pile. Work the background around this stitch before you clip the loops or they will constantly be caught up in your other work.

Turkey Tufting is begun on the *front* side of the canvas in the lower right corner and is worked in horizontal rows back and forth. Do not try to rotate the canvas for this stitch. Turkey Tufting is an excellent special-effects stitch, creating dramatic animal fur, flower centers, and so forth. You can use a single row of Turkey Tufting to fringe the ends of a rug.

Pillow all worked in Turkey Tufting, 17th-century English. The bare spots were caused by deterioration of black yarn dyed with a solution containing iron filings. *Courtesy of the Historic Deerfield Collection, Deerfield, Massachusetts.*

**63**

**TRIANGLE**

1 double strand = 1 sq. in.
1 or more colors
2-3-4-5-4-3-2 count
rotate canvas

Triangle stitch units form a block. This stitch is best worked in quarters, rotating the canvas 90° to work each section. It follows a 2-3-4-5-4-3-2 count. Each corner of the Triangle block can be filled in with a 2 count cross or 4 Tent stitches. Begin the stitch in the lower right corner of your work.

Triangle is very attractive when space is left between the blocks to be filled in with a variety of stitches, such as Brick, Stem, Gobelin Droit or Tent. The Triangle blocks are useful in the corners of borders.

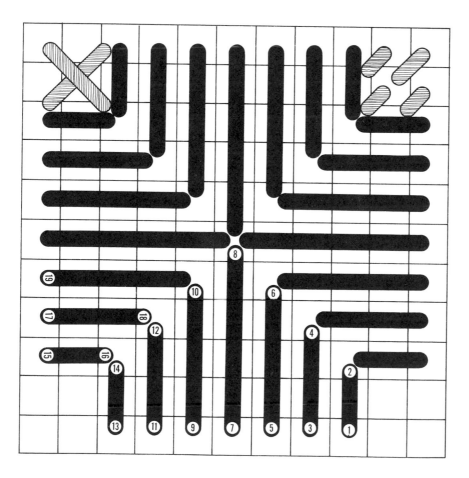

1½ double strands = 1 sq. in.
1 or more colors
3-4 count
do not rotate canvas

Leaf is one of the most striking and popular stitches that is worked on canvas. While each Leaf works up quickly, it is wise to go slowly and count very carefully.

Begin 3 mesh in from the upper right corner of your work. Each side of the stitch begins on the outside and is worked into the center. The first leg goes straight down over 3 mesh. To determine where to begin the next stitch, move down and to the right 1 mesh from where the first stitch began. The next hole (directly beneath the bottom of the first stitch) must *never* be used; leave it open and complete the second stitch in the hole below the empty one.

There are 5 stitches on each side of the Leaf in addition to the top center stitch. When the right side has been completed, begin the left side working up from the bottom. To determine where to begin, move to the left 3 and up 4 mesh from the last stitch (center bottom position). Each stitch joins its "other half" in the center holes.

For all additional Leaves, you will move down 1 mesh rather than having the top of each new stitch share a hole with the row before it. Do not try to rotate the canvas for this stitch.

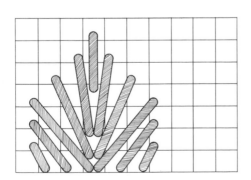

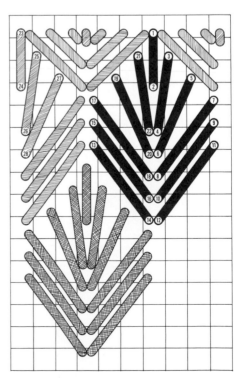

## 65
## RAY
*(Fan)*

2 single strands = 1 sq. in.
1 or more colors
3-3-3-3-2-1-0 count
rotate canvas (90° or 180°)

Ray is basically a square in which all spokes fan out from one corner. It is worked over a 3 mesh square with 7 stitches. Each row can be worked in any direction, and the stitch is effective worked in one or several colors.

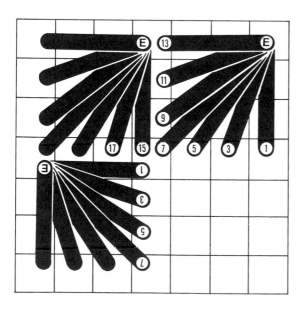

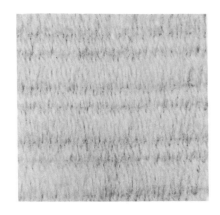

2 single strands = 1 sq. in.
1 color, shade
4-2 or other count
do not rotate canvas

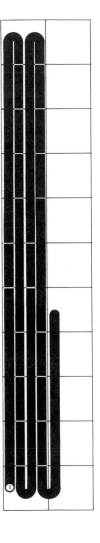

The Darning stitch is a vertical over-and-under stitch that is worked in 4 trips in the same set of holes. Going from bottom to top, go over 4 mesh, under 2, then over 4, and so forth to the edge of the area being covered. On the return from top to bottom, use the same holes, going under 4, over 2 and under 4. Repeat the same procedures up and then down for the third and fourth trips. Move over 1 mesh and repeat all 4 steps.

Other counts can be used instead of the 4-2 formula. An alternative method is to stitch with a double strand, making 2 trips. This stitch has a delicate woven appearance when worked up.

## OVERLAID STITCHES

Overlaid stitches are special decorative stitches that are worked on top of other completed work for further ornamentation. Many of these stitches are used in crewel embroidery, and they are worked in much the same way over canvas. There is no need to follow exact mesh counts in setting the stitches up since they will be worked over finished areas.

If you are left-handed, reverse the order of working spokes and reverse the direction of weaving. Note that Chain stitch (No. 39 on page 87) can be used as a decorative overlaid stitch as well as a regular canvas stitch. Also, Woven Cross (No. 17 on page 65) is used as an overlaid stitch.

## 67
## BACKSTITCH

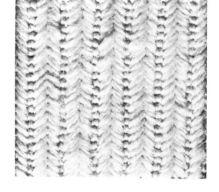

single or double strand
1 color
2-3 or 1-2 count

Backstitching is a very attractive way to finish off an area where canvas shows through between rows of other stitches, such as the Gobelins, for dressing up various canvas stitches like Stem and Leaf or for outlining.

It can be worked over any number of mesh and in any direction. Usually a Backstitch is fairly small; it backs up 1 or 2 mesh on top of the canvas and then is carried ahead underneath 2 or 3 mesh.

## 68
## OUTLINE

single or double strand
1 color
1-2 or 2-3 count

The Outline stitch is especially effective for smoothing out and hiding the vertical and horizontal stepping in curves and diagonal lines.

It is a combination of 2 stitches. The first is a regular running stitch that follows the outer edge of the area to be outlined. Use very short stitches and work them close together with a fairly easy tension. Then loop another strand or 2 of yarn through each of the running stitches. A continuous, tightly twisted line will result, emphasizing the design area.

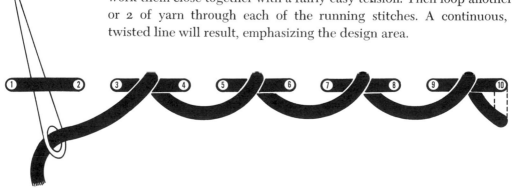

Carol Rome designed and worked the Lamb Pillow in a variety of canvas stitches as a congratulatory baby gift. The sky and butterfly are in Tent, and the treetop is in Leaf. The mountains are in an uneven count Gobelin, and the tree trunk is stitched with Brick. The grass is worked in Stem with Backstitching, the lambs are in Double Straight Cross, and the flowers are made of Ribbed Spiders. The grass in the foreground is in Split Gobelin. Courtesy of Mr. and Mrs. Donald A. Flynn, Seattle.

Mrs. Lynne Fisher of Sea Cliff, N.Y., won an award for this gaily colored pincushion. The top is worked in a Florentine pattern over 27 count canvas, and many canvas stitches adorn the sides. The piece has been photographed here with mirrors to show off all angles of Mrs. Fisher's beautiful work.

Mrs. David Hannah, Jr., and her mother, Mrs. Arthur Coburn, both of Houston, worked this flower rug in sections. The project took several years. The design was worked out by Mrs. Hannah and Bolling Ferris and the stitch used is Diagonal Tent.

This Brick Doorstop Cover by Georgia Devlin shows a novel and attractive use for a sampler. The top of the cover is worked in Tent, Mosaic, Star, Crossed Corners and Vandyke. The side is worked in Tent, Byzantine variation, Diagonal Scotch, and Diagonal Mosaic. The end of the brick is worked in a Florentine pattern.

This director's chair is worked in stripes on 5 count canvas. It was designed to match a pair of window shades. Carol Rome.

Rosemary Nicol Smith of Fort Lauderdale, Fla., worked this beautiful 9½' x 8½' rug over 10 count canvas with the help of Bobbie Rosier. Mrs. Smith and her friend planned the design of wild ducks and cattails, and Karen Walter worked out the design details. A rug of this size is a major undertaking, but the end results are well worth the time spent.

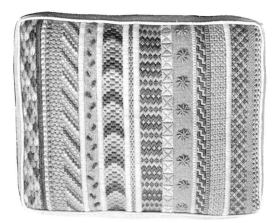

Carol Rome worked this sampler over 16 count canvas. The row of flowers was created with overstitched French Knots, and Ribbed Spiders decorate a strip of Tent stitch. Even if you have no great drawing ability, you can make an attractive needle-point design just by using combinations of colors and different canvas stitches. The texture created is pleasing and speaks "embroidery."

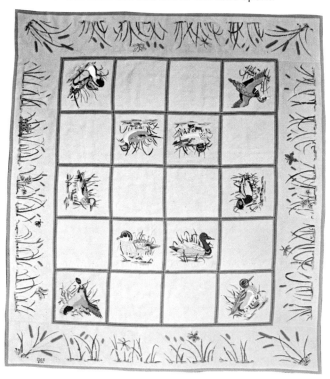

double strand
1 color
forward under 2, back over 1

Ribbed Spiders are delightful! They demand touching and make beautiful, textured accents over other canvas stitches. First set up a "wheel" that has 8 spokes that are worked through the canvas covering approximately 4 to 6 mesh. On completing the eighth spoke, bring the needle to the front of the canvas between any 2 spokes as close to the center as possible. The next operation is to weave around the spokes *on top* of the canvas.

Proceed clockwise, going back *over* 1 spoke and forward *under* 2 spokes. This weaving is continued around and around the spokes until they are filled in snuggly. The last time you back up, take the needle straight through to the back of the canvas and end the thread in the usual way.

Keep the tension tighter in the center while weaving and ease up as you work outward to keep the spokes from "bending" as they radiate outward.

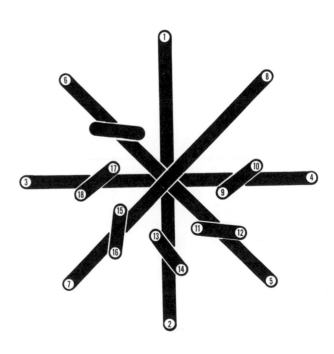

## 70
## RAISED SPIDER
*(Woven Spider)*

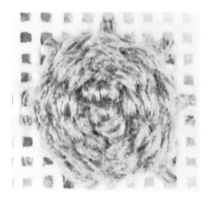

double strand
1 color
over 1, under 1

The Raised Spider has an odd number of spokes. It is set up exactly the same as the Ribbed Spider except that the sixth spoke is placed closer to the first spoke. Come to the front of the canvas between spokes 6 and 4. Next slide the needle under the spokes without going through to the underside of the canvas and come out between spokes 3 and 5.

Before you pull the needle all the way through, loop the yarn up over it and then pull the needle through. A small knot will result as well as the extra seventh spoke. Pull up on the knotted thread and weave the spokes by going clockwise over 1 spoke and then under the next. There is no backing up. Again, keep the tension tighter toward the middle and looser as you work outward.

double strand
1 color
forward over 2, back under 1

The Rosette is a variation of the Ribbed Spider. First set up 8 equidistant spokes over approximately 4 to 6 mesh. Come out close to the center between 2 spokes. The spokes are woven clockwise, going back under 1 and forward over 2.

Weave around and around until all the spokes are filled out. The last time you go forward over 2, take the yarn to the back of the canvas and end it.

# 72
# LIFESAVER

double strand
1 color
over 1, under 1

The Lifesaver is another Spider variation. Set up an 8-spoke wheel and come out close to the center between 2 spokes. Begin to weave these spokes clockwise going over 1 and then under 1. There is no backing up. Because there is an even number of spokes, 4 spokes will always be under the woven yarn and 4 spokes always will be on top.

# FRENCH KNOT

double strand
1 color

French Knots are one of the embroiderer's best friends! They can be used singly or in groups for all sorts of attractive effects. They make excellent flower centers and accents and can create a nubby texture when worked in clusters over a large area.

To make a French Knot, secure the yarn on the underside of the canvas and come through to the front. Holding the needle with your right hand, wrap the yarn over and around the needle 1, 2 or 3 times, depending on how big you want the knot to be. Pull the yarn fairly taut on the needle and then poke the needle through to the backside of the canvas, ending the strand or carrying it over to the location of the next French Knot. The wrapped yarn will "pile up" on the surface of the canvas into a tiny, tight knot.

Left-handed stitchers should hold the needle in their left hand and wrap the yarn with the right hand.

## 74

## GOBELIN DROIT VARIATION

The Gobelin Droit variation uses varying lengths of upright stitches in an even or uneven progression. It can be worked over any count. However, remember—the longer the stitch the more easily it will snag.

## 75

## BRICK VARIATION

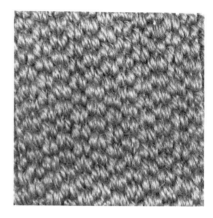

In this variation, the Brick is doubled or worked in pairs of stitches over a 2-2-3 count; 3 mesh are left between each pair for the alternate rows to fit in.

## 76

## OLD FLORENTINE VARIATION

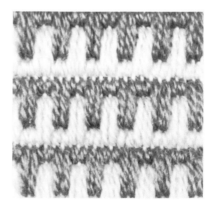

This variation has a 2-2-6-6 count. Both the long and the short stitches end at the same place at one edge. The second row interlocks evenly with the first.

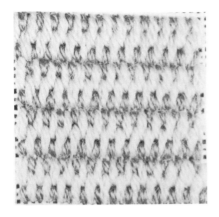

## 77
## PARISIAN VARIATION

To work the Parisian variation, make 2 interlocking rows of the long stitches and then fill in with 2 rows of the short stitches.

## 78
## HUNGARIAN VARIATION

This variation creates a continuous horizontal row of diamonds that fit in with the Florentine patterns. After completing each unit over a 2-4-6-4-2 count, move over 2 mesh and repeat the grouping.

## 79
## ST. ANDREW—ST. GEORGE
### (Reversed Double Cross)

This is a variation on Smyrna. The crosses are worked alternately, first with the straight cross (St. George) on top and then with the diagonal cross (St. Andrew) on top. Both crosses are worked over a 4-4 count with a full strand.

## 80
## STAR VARIATION
*(Eye)*

This variation, sometimes called Eye, is very similar to the Star except it has 16 instead of 8 stitches going into the center hole. A single strand is sufficient to cover the canvas. Each stitch is worked over a 2 count.

(opposite)

Tree Trunk by Mrs. Henry Swift, Columbus, Georgia. This lovely piece combines crewel stitches with canvas stitches to form "crewelpoint." Note the subtle shading and modeling that can be achieved by using these two types of embroidery together.

# CHAPTER 4

A geometric Swedish design worked
from a chart by Mrs. Grant D. Ross,
Denver. Designed by Lillill Thane.

# Easy Lessons
# in Design

This detail from the Wedding Pillow by Carol Rome (shown in color on frontispiece)
shows the rich texture that is created by the use of a combination of canvas stitches.

# IF YOU'RE GOING TO BUY A KIT

When shopping for a ready-made kit, there are several things to consider in making sure you are getting your money's worth. First of all, avoid buying a fill-in-the-background kit unless it is purely for the sake of practicing a new background stitch. It simply isn't worth the amount of care and time you will be investing; the work becomes downright boring and may turn you against doing another project for weeks!

Look at the canvas carefully. Make sure enough room has been left on all sides so that blocking can be done easily. Preferably there should be 1½″ blank canvas around the designed area; however 1″ will do. The canvas should be stiff and shiny and free of knots or weak spots, and the canvas edges should be securely taped or hemmed.

The kit should contain either Persian or tapestry yarn that is soft and lustrous. Watch out for kits that call for the use of Half Cross or Continental stitch. Less yarn may be included in these kits than is needed to work Diagonal Tent, and you may come up short.

Some kit manufacturers are not careful about matching the colors of the packaged yarn to the colors that are marked on the canvas. In some cases, if the stitches do not cover the canvas completely, the painted color will show through, detracting from the appearance of the finished piece. If possible, find out what has been used to paint the canvas; it must be completely colorfast or you can expect disaster during blocking.

Kits come with the design marked in a variety of ways. Many canvases are traméed, with strands of the designated colors worked over each area. Still other kits contain a color chart in which outlined areas have numbers corresponding to a numbered list of colors. If your kit design is on graph paper, chances are the squares are colored in, giving a fairly realistic idea of the finished product. When you are working with the graphed design, remember that the squares really represent canvas mesh or stitches rather than holes or you will have trouble counting.

Scene of Lynmouth, Devonshire, England, worked from a chart. The canvas was traméed before stitching. Mrs. John C. Stears, Denver, designed by Stitchcraft, Ltd.

Many canvas designs are hand-painted. Generally, these canvases are the best quality, and more time and care has gone into their manufacture. As a result, the kits are correspondingly higher priced.

Beware of kits that contain silkscreened canvases. This is a method of mass-producing designs by a stenciling process, and frequently the pattern is laid down off the true grain of the canvas. If you get a canvas that is silkscreened off-grain, no amount of pulling or blocking can put the design back on grain. Take the kit back, and next time check (with a ruler, if necessary) to make sure all vertical and horizontal lines in the design match *exactly* the vertical and horizontal mesh of the canvas.

Look at the kit price tag and compute this cost with the cost of having the project blocked and mounted, if you are not planning to do this yourself. You should know before you start to work whether you want to make such an investment. Some kits may not be expensive in themselves but are very expensive to make up; notably, handbags that require hardware, vests, slippers, telephone book covers, tennis racquet covers and director's chairs. Make sure you get firm quotes on finishing charges before you buy the kit.

Now that you have selected a kit that meets your needs and is pleasing in design and colors, you can start thinking about the stitching. This brings us to some hints on how to "doctor" a kit to make it all your own.

## HOW TO PERSONALIZE A KIT

There are a variety of ways to personalize a needlepoint kit. If you are feeling timid, you can work the design and background areas in Diagonal Tent. Then add a pretty border of your own design, something simple with good texture that will frame the work and add dimension to the piece. Remember that you must allow at least 1″ (preferably 1½″) blank margins for blocking, so you may have to borrow some of the design background

Christmas tree kit worked with a border. The background is French stitch, and French Knots have been added to make the holly. Mrs. Robert B. Crouch, Houston. Designed by Designs for You.

The same Christmas tree kit with a Diagonal Tent background. This time the tree is worked in Leaf stitch with French knots, and Smyrna has been used in the border. Mrs. Robert B. Crouch, Houston. Designed by Designs for You.

area for your border. When you are finished, you may be inspired to add a few French Knots or an Outline stitch to the design using leftover yarn, embroidery floss or metal thread.

Now that you are feeling more confident, try working the background in a simple stitch like Hungarian, Old Florentine or Brick. You will be surprised how much added depth the use of a different stitch for the background can give your finished piece. Another bonus in using one of these stitches is that the work moves along much more quickly than with Diagonal Tent, and before you know it, you'll be ready to start a new project.

Tricks with color can enhance the look of a kit design. Mix strands of different colors in the needle and work them in together to create shading or a tweedy effect. It is also possible to create shadows by repeating the design elements in darker shades several mesh over and down from the original design.

The next kit you work may end up a masterpiece of ingenuity. It will have an attractive border, several different stitches used in the design and background, some decorative overstitching, perhaps a few color variations, *and* a well-proportioned monogram to sign the piece. Your sense of personal accomplishment and pride is swelling at this point. The next logical step is designing your own canvas.

## DESIGNING YOUR OWN CANVAS

How many times have you told yourself that you have no artistic talent and have no business making up your own canvas designs? How many times have you searched through kits to find something that resembles the idea

This flower design is worked in several different stitches, giving the piece texture and depth. Georgia Devlin. Designed by Merribee.

Frog pillow by Karen Kirkpatrick, Houston. Designed by Merribee.

Scythian horseman by Mary Cooke Woodward, Washington, D.C. The design for this pillow was inspired by an ancient wall painting.

in your mind and had to compromise either with the pattern or the colors? How many times have you seen "your" pillow in someone else's home?

*Anyone* can make a design and transfer the pattern to canvas, and there are many reasons why you should try. First of all, the amount of work you will put into any piece of needlepoint warrants individuality and uniqueness. A finished article should reflect your own personal taste and interests. In addition, the only way to control the quality of raw materials going into your work is to choose them yourself. You will know what has been used to mark the canvas, and you won't have to worry about it during blocking. You can pick out the colors and choose exactly what you want. In addition, you will save money.

## SOURCES OF DESIGN

Your next question may be, "I can't draw, so where do I find design ideas?" It may not have occurred to you that designing involves a whole series of decisions about color placement, raw materials, size and texture. If you have added just one personal touch to a ready-made kit, you have been designing!

The first place to look for design ideas is to the stitches themselves. From the stitches of canvas embroidery spring a boundless wealth of patterns. Putting two or three together in stripes makes a design that can easily stand on its own. Designing with color and stitches does not require any drawing ability, but rather a sense of balance and texture. The cover of this book is a good example of the effectiveness of designing with stitches.

The patterns you create with combinations of stitches are considered geometric designs. The interest lies in the repeated blocks, triangles, lines or circles of color and texture that the stitches make up. Further sources of

Pillow worked in Diagonal Tent with a repeat pattern of Leaf and Scotch stitch by Mrs. Paul Cohen, Albany.

Symmetrical Geometric Sampler by Karyn H. Katz, Brooklyn. Mrs. Katz worked out the design using combinations of stitches as she went along.

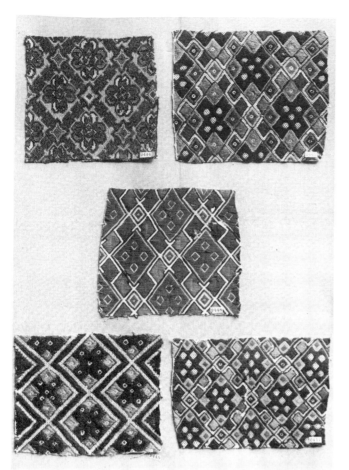

Fragments of embroidery in geometric designs; Albanian or Montenegrin, 18th and 19th centuries. *Courtesy of The Metropolitan Museum of Art, Rogers Fund, 1909.*

Square Sampler by Mrs. Ben Marcus, Milwaukee. This lovely piece is a series of frames worked in different stitches and should give you good ideas for decorative borders.

American or English chair seat cover, second half of the 18th century, worked in Cross stitch in a repeat geometric design. *Courtesy of Bayou Bend Collection, The Museum of Fine Arts, Houston.*

This bench seat was finished in 1745 by Sarah Richardson in England according to the signature on the piece. The repeat design of fan-shaped palmettes in shaded colors outlined in dark brown has attractive, flowing lines. *Courtesy of the Colonial Williamsburg Foundation.*

ideas for geometric designs include wallpaper, wrapping paper, tile catalogs, fabric and abstract art.

You won't necessarily want to limit your design repertoire to geometrics. Look around you for a drawing or photograph that resembles your concept of a design you would like to stitch. You may find it in your china pattern, on a postcard or poster, in a book or magazine, in a museum painting or on a silk scarf.

Your inspiration may have come from a piece of antique china in your living room or the oriental carpet in the hall. The four seasons, signs of the Zodiac, activities of the twelve months, personal hobbies, family trees, and scenes from nature have been depicted in canvas embroidery for centuries. Before you go any farther in planning your design, keep in mind that you are working with a medium that has its own special advantages and limitations.

The design for this cushion was inspired by a china pattern. Mary Conrad White, Gates Mills, Ohio. Designed by Martha Wick.

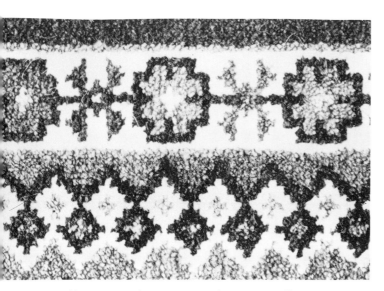

Your oriental carpet can be an excellent source of design.

Some plants lend themselves very well to needlepoint. These delicate blossoms would work up well in French Knots.

This address book cover design matches the wallpaper in color and pattern. Lé Stitcherie, Houston.

## NEEDLEPOINT AS A MEDIUM

Canvas embroidery, from time immemorial, has been a decorative art in which color, texture and craftsmanship are blended together to enhance the beauty of a place or object. It is wise to remember that you will lose some of the special quality of this medium if you try to force your needle and yarns to do what paintbrush and oils or a camera have achieved. When you find a design that you like from one of the hundreds of readily available sources around you, keep in mind that the finished needlepoint piece very likely will not look exactly the same as the original design.

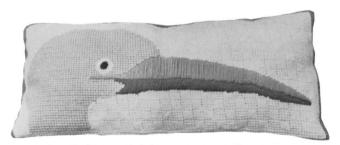

These birds by Jean Kommel of Roslyn, N.Y., have been treated simply, allowing the texture of the stitches to become a focal point of interest.

When translated from art or photography into needlepoint, the design will lose some of its detail and modeling. This is due mainly to the canvas "ground" over which the stitches are worked. The canvas mesh form a grid that necessitates stepping free flowing curves and diagonal straight lines into a series of tiny right angles. (The smaller the canvas gauge, the less angular the curves will appear and the more detail you can include in the design.)

Subjects should be treated more simply than pictorially, allowing the inherent beauty of the yarn colors and stitch texture to illuminate the finished work. It has often been said that a finished needlepoint piece is a failure if it is mistaken for a painting. It is a far better compliment to have your work recognized as a fine example of embroidery.

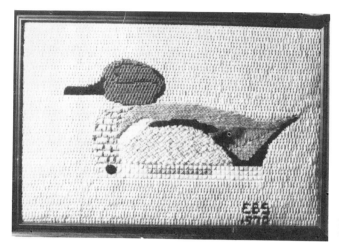

Mrs. Donald Schmidt, Jr., of Milwaukee has been able to achieve some modeling in her duck decoys through the use of stitches and color. These birds were designed by Dr. Frank Belfus.

## BASICS OF DESIGN

The first major consideration is the destination and use of the finished piece. You will want the article to blend in with its surroundings in color, formality and subject matter while remaining a unique adornment.

The elements of design you should consider are proportion, balance, movement and rhythm. A small center design floating on a large background will look unimportant and boring. On the other hand, an overcrowded canvas or one in which the scale of the design is too big for the piece will be confusing to the eye. Your eye should stay on the canvas and

"Artichokes" by Mrs. Harry Powell Wilson, Jr., Denver. This piece is literally tied together by bows, giving a feeling of movement and rhythm to the design.

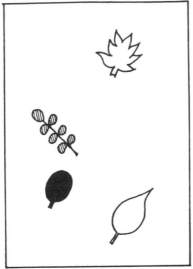

is design is too small for the space
lotted. The dotted line indicates a
ore suitable size-space relationship.

This design is scattered and unrhythmical. Too much blank space
has been left.

The same design elements scaled
larger and overlapped make a
more interesting, related arrangement.

is shell is too large for the allotted
ace. Also, its round contours would
ok better in a circular area.

This design is well balanced and has the right propor-
tions for the allotted space. The curved lines give movement and rhythm to the design.

move around within the design. Lines slanting toward the edge may lead
the eye off the canvas, and a scattered, unrhythmical design will leave you
with a negative impression.

One of the best ways to experiment with these basic design elements is
to make several paper cutouts of flowers, leaves or random shapes and
then move these around on a piece of background paper into different
arrangements. You may come up with a pleasing design by this method,
and you will not have had to pick up a pencil!

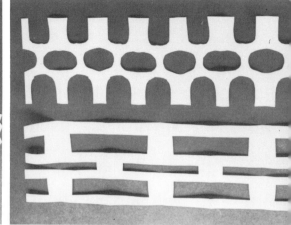

Cut-paper designs.

## BASICS OF COLOR

Knowing the organization of colors by groups may help you in selecting a color scheme for a needlepoint project. The primary colors in the color-wheel are red, blue and yellow. Combinations of these primaries make up the secondary colors, which are green, orange and violet. (Blue and yellow make green, red and yellow make orange, and red and blue make violet.) All other color or hue variations come from combinations of the primary and secondary colors. Shades of a color are made by adding black. Tints are made by adding white. Brown is made by mixing complementary primary and secondary colors such as red with green. You can see that several color families branch out from the primary colors and that there are many variations of shades and tints of each color within the families.

We tend to associate various colors with feelings or moods. Yellows, oranges and reds are considered bright, happy and hot. They tend to pop out from a surface to catch the eye. Greens, blues and violets are serene and cool. They seem to recede into a surface. Grays and browns are the neutral colors.

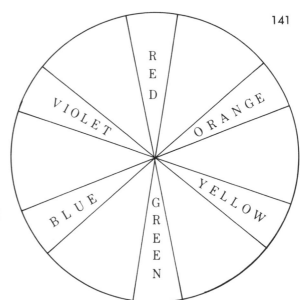

The basic color wheel. Opposite primary and secondary colors are complementary.

No matter how well your design is balanced and positioned on the canvas, it will not come alive until color has been added. The first thing to remember is to limit the number of colors you use on a given piece to avoid fussiness and confusion. Consider again the destination of the finished piece. The colors should be bold enough to make the piece stand out but not so bold that the surrounding objects appear dull and nondescript. In the best designs, colors are harmoniously arranged to compliment each other and the subject of the design in addition to fitting in with the setting of the room.

There are very few restrictions placed on color schemes these days. Colors that seem to "go together" now would have been considered outlandish ten years ago. A wall hanging of purple cats with pink polka dots for a child's room is no less suitable than a pair of traditional deep red slippers with a white monogram.

When working out a color scheme, make sure that you have not overloaded one area of the canvas with bright colors or your eye will stop on this spot in the design. Bold, bright colors come on strong and may need toning down and balancing with a few neutral or quiet colors to make the design work well. Keep in mind that all colors will look slightly darker when stitched.

If you want an object to look realistic, you will use several shades and tints of one color for modeling. The light color will be toward the center of the object with gradations of shading getting darker toward the edges. The same principle holds true if you want to create a realistic perspective in a scene. The light colors should be worked into the foreground with darker colors receding into the distance.

This apple has been broken down into several color areas to create realistic modeling.

## METHODS

There are many methods of getting designs onto the canvas, starting with the most elementary, which is simply to design as you go along, putting together different combinations of stitches. This does not require any marking of the canvas except the outside dimensions and center vertical and horizontal lines, which can be applied with a pencil.

*Tracing:* The next easiest method is to make a direct tracing onto canvas from a picture, photograph, piece of fabric, your child's artwork or whatever you have chosen as your design source. (Sometimes you will put together a combination of subjects from different sources.) You should mark off vertical and horizontal center lines on the canvas for reference during the tracing process and for convenience during blocking later on. If the vertical and horizontal lines on the canvas seem slightly cockeyed and don't intersect at right angles, it may mean that the canvas is slightly off-grain. Pull the canvas diagonally until the lines are on true grain.

Lay the canvas on top of the picture and tape or clip it in place. Then trace with an *indelible* marking pen or pencil. Gray or another fairly light neutral color is easier on the eyes than black and is less apt to show through

| | |
|---|---|
| An art poster of Odilon Redon's *Large Green Vase,* Museum of Fine Arts, Boston, is used for a wall hanging design. | A direct tracing is made on 24 count mono canvas from the art poster. Use a very fine brush for tracing. |

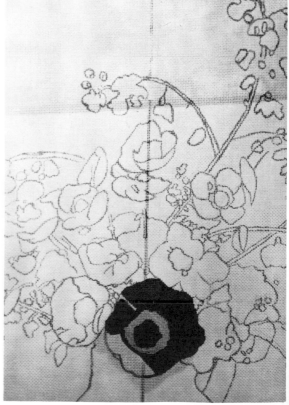

the stitching later on. If you are making a tracing from a library book or any other book you don't want to mar, place a sheet of clear acetate between the page and the canvas.

If you are having trouble seeing through the canvas to the picture underneath, work on a glass-topped table with a strong light beneath or tape the pieces to a window. Very often, making a preliminary tracing on tracing paper and underlining this with white paper makes the work easier.

Tracings have been made from scenes of nature and are ready to transfer to canvas.

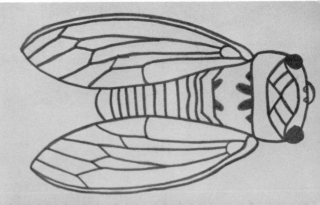

Tracings also can be made of shapes you have cut from paper or out of magazines and newspapers. In many cases, you will be combining elements from two or three sources into a new arrangement in your design. It is always best to experiment on tracing paper rather than the canvas for the obvious reason that you can erase marks from the paper more easily than from the canvas.

*Photostats:* You may find a design idea that is exactly what you want except it is the wrong size. You can have the design enlarged or reduced by having photostats made according to your specifications. This is not very expensive and should take just one or two days. Photostating is a photographic process that results first in a negative photostat (all the lines you want will be white, and the background will be black) and then in a positive. Ask for a positive because it is difficult to work from the negative copy.

Wallpaper by Eaglesham is inspiration for a design.

Tracings are made of the main design elements.

Negative and then positive photostats are made of the tracings, reducing the size in half.

The photostats are placed under another piece of tracing paper, and a design is made from a new arrangement of the design elements. The design is ready to transfer to canvas.

*Adding Color:* Many people prefer to work with a canvas that has the design areas outlined but not colored in. This gives them the option of developing the color scheme as they proceed, occasionally changing colors from the original plan.

However, there are also good reasons for painting the colors on the canvas. First of all, you can be virtually assured that no areas of white or tan canvas will show through in the finished piece since the canvas will be the same color as the stitched yarn. Also, you can see exactly how the color scheme will look in finished form, possibly saving you from errors in judgment.

The easiest working method is to use two tracings. The first tracing is marked in black outlines only, delineating the design areas. This is placed beneath the canvas. The second tracing is outlined and has the colors added in. Place this beside you for reference as you work. It is not necessary to outline the design areas on the canvas. All that is needed is to paint on the colors, using the outlines as a guide.

Two tracings are used when painting in the color areas on canvas. The outline tracing is placed under the canvas, and the colored-in tracing is kept on hand for reference.

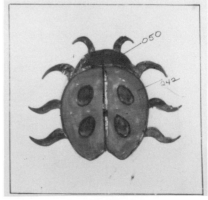

*Paints and Markers:* One of the hottest debates in needlepoint today is what should be used to paint the canvas. Using the wrong material can end in disaster when the canvas is blocked after stitching. Innumerable pieces have been completely ruined by having the paints bleed when they were wet. There is no one answer except to say that whatever you use should be absolutely colorfast.

The following is a list of the more popular materials.

1. Oil paint has been used to paint canvases traditionally. It may need to be thinned with turpentine. Some people add Japan Dryer to the paint to speed drying time. Still, to be safe, wait 48 hours before stitching.

2. Textile paints, such as those manufactured by Prang, are preferred by many people. The colors must be mixed with an extender before use. Textile paints are completely colorfast *after* they have dried and have been set with a hot iron. (Place a damp cloth between the iron and canvas when setting the colors.)

3. Acrylic paints have become more popular in recent years. These apply in much the same way that oils apply; however, acrylic paint is water soluble and can be thinned with water.

4. An increasing number of professionals are using Flo-paque paints, which come in small bottles and dry very quickly. The colors can be used "straight"; however, the color range is limited so that a good deal of mixing is necessary.

5. Still other designers use the Studio Magic Marker felt-tipped pens for marking the canvas. Most of these markers have blunt ends which may have to be trimmed to a point for use in small areas or as an outliner.

*Hints on Painting:* No matter what kind of paint or marker you decide to use, avoid using excessive amounts of these materials or you will clog the canvas and come through to the underside. Be sure the paint is fully dry before you begin to stitch the piece. Match the paint colors as closely to the yarn colors as you can, keeping the canvas colors slightly subdued so they won't show through the stitches.

Be sure whatever you use to paint the canvas is permanent and colorfast. A patch test doesn't take much time and can save you disappointment and loss of time and money.

Be kind to your paint brushes and materials. Brushes should be kept clean and dry, the bristles reshaped to a point after each use. Bottle and tube caps of all paints should be given an extra twist to make sure they are on tight, otherwise your paints will evaporate or dry up. Magic Marker pen caps should be replaced immediately after you are finished with each color.

*Working with the Canvas Grid:* The direct tracing methods described above do not take into consideration the necessary stepping of curves and diagonal lines into a series of right angles. You will find when examining your painted canvas that rounded outlines sometimes pass over mesh and other times pass over holes. For a while, you will have to select by trial and error the starting point for each new stitch that conforms most closely to the "ideal" outline. A few stitches can be added later to round out a curve that looks slightly moth-eaten.

At other times, you may be stymied by a diagonal design line that does not exactly match the bias or diagonal grain of the canvas. You will not be able to execute a perfectly straight line, but will have to make stitch groupings that follow the design line as closely as possible. When the piece is finished and you stand back to look at it, the diagonal line will appear to be unbroken.

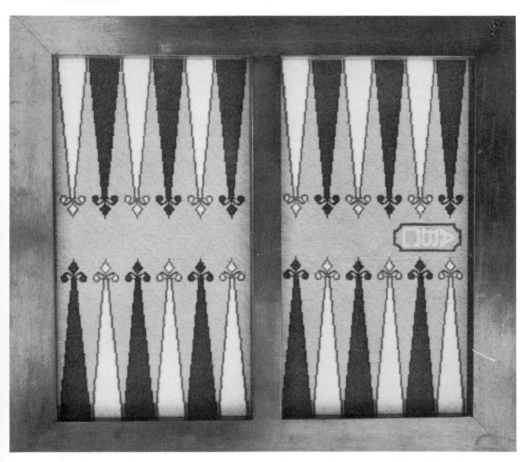

Backgammon board by Mrs. Anthony B. Cudahy, Omaha. Designed by Mili Holmes. Notice the regular grouping of stitches to form the "off-grain" diagonal lines in this effective, simple design.

On occasion you will work an area of fine detail on Penelope canvas within areas of full-size stitching. After the detail areas have been stitched in Tent, you may notice that there are some bare canvas mesh that the background stitches won't cover. In this case, fill in around the detail area with additional half-size Tent stitches of the background color.

The Union Jack posed a problem with diagonal lines. Again, the stitches have been grouped following the diagonals as closely as possible. Carol Rome.

Stitch the design areas first before working on the background. You may decide to change the design somewhat after you have started. If the background is already filled in, you will not be able to "move" outlines without ripping out background stitching. Also, many people change their minds about background colors and stitches after the design has been worked.

*Designing with Graph Paper:* Some designs demand exact counting to make them work on canvas. This is especially true of designs that contain

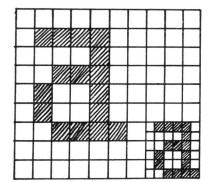

A freehand letter "a" is graphed and then enlarged on graph paper with bigger blocks.

repeat linear motifs, any kind of lettering or numbering or complex border patterns. A freehand tracing of a motto most likely would result in unevenly spaced, crooked letters no matter how competent the designer might be. Graph paper is the most effective tool for working out these designs since it exactly matches the canvas grid.

A design worked out on graph paper.

As mentioned earlier in the section on kits, graph paper designs can be terribly confusing when the blocks are marked in with color. Your first inclination is to think of the blocks as canvas *holes* rather than mesh, and

A graphed design with charted colors. The blank squares indicate one color, the black boxes a second color, and the X-ed boxes a third color.

this is where the trouble begins. If you think of the graph paper blocks as canvas mesh, your design will come out without extra or missing rows of stitching. If this still seems confusing, mark the graph paper lines with individual stitches to get an exact replica of the canvas. You can enlarge a graph paper design by working the same design on graph paper that has larger squares.

The graph paper can be painted with the colors you are planning to use, or you can chart the colors with symbols, using the graph paper design as a reference while stitching the canvas. The only lines that need be marked directly on the canvas are the vertical and horizontal center lines and the outside dimensions. The rest is a matter of very careful counting.

## LETTERING IN NEEDLEPOINT

For centuries, lettering has been an integral part of embroidery designs, used not only as explanation of the embroidered scene, but as an added decoration. When using letters or numbers in needlepoint, consider them as elements of the design that must harmonize in style, size and placement with the other subject matter.

You may want to work a motto or decorative alphabet, and there will be many times when a monogram will be part of your finished piece. Be very careful to work out each letter you are planning to use and the letter spacing before attempting to stitch the canvas. Working with graph paper is the most successful way of constructing the letters and getting them evenly spaced.

Numbers worked in different stitches make up this design. Slightly different styles have been used. Remember to graph letters and numbers before working them on canvas. Mrs. Robert B. Crouch, Houston, designed by Esther Feldman.

## BORDER DESIGNS

A border is the most attractive way to frame your needlepoint work. Many borders are worked in Diagonal Tent in repeat designs that harmonize with the major design of the piece. Other borders are made up of combinations of various needlepoint stitches in repeat sequences.

Turning the corner occasionally poses a problem of logistics that can be easily solved with the use of a pocketbook mirror. Work the design on graph paper and then place a small mirror diagonally across the border design at a place that seems suitable for turning so that the design is reflected at right angles. Use the reflection as a guide in starting the next side. If you prefer, you can make a tracing of your border design. Make a second tracing from the wrong side of the original. Put the two together at right angles, folding back the corners to diagonals. A diagonal line drawn from the inside perimeter to the outside perimeter of a border at the corners is usually a sufficient guide when the border is composed of stitch combinations.

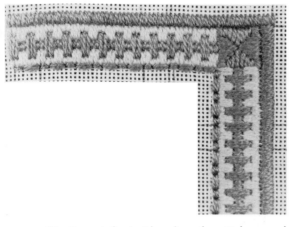

Starting at the inside edge, the stitches used are Darning, Old Florentine, and Gobelin Droit.

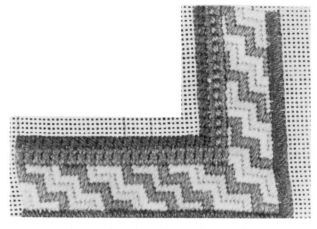

Starting at the inside edge, the stitches used are Mosaic, Oblong with Backstitch, Byzantine, and Gobelin Oblique.

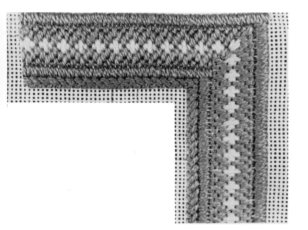

Starting at the inside edge, the stitches used are Vandyke, Gobelin Oblique, Hungarian Ground, and Gobelin Droit.

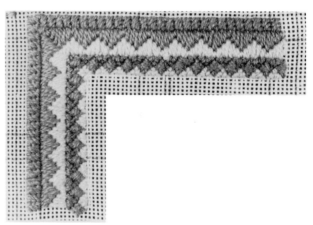

Starting at the inside edge, the stitches used are Double Straight Cross, a Triangle variation, and Cashmere.

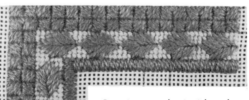

Starting at the inside edge, the stitches used are Gobelin Droit, Leaf with a Tent background, and Flat.

These borders were designed by Georgia Devlin.

Make sure that your border design does not overpower the main design. You may have to add a few extra rows of Tent around the outside of the border to sacrifice in the mounting process if you want the whole border to show in the finished piece.

A striped sampler started with a border using Gobelin Droit and Old Florentine. Triangle has been used in three corners — the bottom right corner has been left free for a monogram. Carol Rome.

# CHAPTER 5

# Projects

This delightful Santa Claus Christmas ornament is enhanced by the use of French Knots for the fur of the hat, Straight Cross for the hat, Split Gobelin for the beard, and Encroaching Oblique for the mustache. Santa's face and the background are worked in Tent. Mrs. William Whitcroft, Milwaukee, designed by Subo.

## INTRODUCTION

This chapter explains how to set up and finish twenty-three projects that lend themselves particularly well to needlepoint. These projects fall into two large groups: personal accessories and household furnishings. You may be surprised to find how simple it is to mount many of these items. In some cases, you need only some glue and poster board. Other projects require hand-sewing or the use of a sewing machine for finishing. Still others are best mounted professionally.

The notes in this chapter will be useful to you whether you plan to mount your work at home or have it sent off to be professionally mounted. Suggested canvas gauges, dimensions and proper methods of measuring the projects are presented. Hints about planning the design are given so your pattern won't come out upside down or sideways when the piece is mounted. The instructions on finishing will give you a firm knowledge of various mounting processes so you can do the job yourself and can develop a sense of quality control for the pieces you pay to have finished.

This chapter should serve as an inspiration for the many items you can make by hand for yourself or home and to give as gifts. Many projects can be stitched and made up in a short time and without a great deal of expense. No doubt lots of ideas for items not mentioned here will come to mind for your next project. Go ahead—make it! Remember two things: always block the piece carefully after stitching and always get a firm estimate on charges for finishing before you send a piece to be mounted professionally. Find out whether the charges include blocking or if this is a separate charge. Your local needlework specialty shop can be of great assistance with those pieces that you want professionally mounted.

Karen Kirkpatrick of Houston made these pincushions with napkin rings. The 4½" circular pieces of needlepoint are glued in place inside the rings and padded with foam rubber. The pincushion holding pins is worked in rows of Gobelin Droit over different counts. Proceeding clockwise, the stitches used are Tent in a plaid pattern, Diagonal Cashmere, Tent with an initial (the small pincushion) and a Florentine pattern. The pincushion in the middle is worked in a zigzag pattern of Gobelin Droit in alternating long and short rows.

A Florentine pattern in shaded pinks is worked in a strip to make a belt. The edges were finished with the binding stitch, a grosgrain ribbon lining was blind stitched to the back, and frog closures were tacked in place. Georgia Devlin.

## PERSONAL ACCESSORIES                                     1

### BELTS AND CUMMERBUNDS

A belt or cummerbund project is a good way to make use of leftover strips of canvas. It is a project that can be worked up quickly and makes a fine, personal gift.

Take the waist measurement and add ½" extra stitching room to either end for ease. The width of the belt is a matter of personal preference, 1½" to 3" being the most popular widths for women's belts. Add the usual 1½" blank margin on all 4 sides before cutting the canvas. Tape or hem the canvas edges.

Center and mark the finished outline size on the canvas and apply your design if you plan to use one, or create a pattern with combinations of stitches as you go. After stitching is completed, block as usual.

1. Press-on Pellon can be applied to the wrong side of the work to add body and stability. To secure the mesh and to prevent raveling, machine-stitch 3 times about ¼" outside the worked area all around the canvas.

2. If you are using the binding stitch, turn the unworked margin to the wrong side. Trim the excess to ½" and miter the corners. Tack the unworked margins loosely in place, press and hammer the corners flat. Then bind all 4 sides and add a pretty strip of backing by hand using a blindstitch.

3. If you are using a sewing machine, put the backing strip with the needlepoint, right sides together. Stitch twice around 3 sides for added strength. Turn right side out and blindstitch the fourth side closed by hand.

4. Add rings, frogs, large hooks and eyes or Velcro tabs for the closure. (If using Velcro, plan to allow for a 3" overlap when measuring the canvas and planning the design.)

*Notes on the Traditional Man's Belt:* First buy a buckle with a leather tab and an accompanying leather tab with punched holes at a notions store. Also purchase the proper length of belting, which will be used to back the piece. Take the actual waist measurement and add 1" stitching room for ease. The

Orient the design on the suspenders vertically.

resulting measurement gives you the length of belting needed. The width is determined by the width of the leather tab. The needlepoint belt should be the same width as the tab.

After blocking, the unworked edges of the needlepoint are turned under, pressed flat and whipped down. The belting is machine-stitched to the back between the first and second rows of needlepoint work. The buckle and punched tab are machine-stitched in place last.

*Notes on Suspenders:* Buy the hardware first, using the width of the hardware to gauge the width of the needlepoint strips. For length, measure from waist over the shoulder to waist on each side, allowing an extra ½″ stitching room at all 4 ends for ease plus the usual 1½″ blank margin on all sides. Remember to orient the design up and down rather than sideways on the canvas strips. Representational designs should be worked out so that the motifs meet head-on in the middle of the strips or half the design will be upside down when the suspenders are worn. Finish the suspenders according to the instructions for belts and cummerbunds.

# 2
## CASES

A personalized case for glasses, rain hat and various other necessities is a lovely accessory to own or give as a gift. These projects are small and, therefore, do not take long to work up. All cases finish out better when made from one piece of canvas. The finer the canvas gauge, the prettier the case will be (14 count and smaller is recommended). When planning the design, keep in mind which way the case will be folded. For instance, a vertical design on a glasses case should be worked out so that the bottoms of the design are next to the fold.

Cut the canvas to the suggested dimensions or to dimensions you calculate, adding 1½″ on all sides as a blank margin. Tape or hem the canvas edges and apply the design. Stitch and block the piece as usual.

### Glasses Case

A case measuring 3½″ x 13″ will fit most glasses, but check yours individually. Orient the design with the bottoms of the pattern next to the center fold. Finish in either way.

Don't make this mistake! When the case is mounted, the designs will come out upside down.

Georgia Devlin created a plaid pattern for this glasses case using Brick for the background, Tent for the wide stripes, and Gobelin Oblique for the narrow stripes. The binding stitch was used to finish the edges of the case.

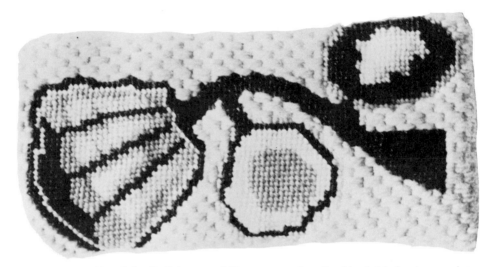

Mrs. John F. Schwarz of Houston used a Double Brick background to achieve texture in her stylized floral design. Tent was used for the flower on this glasses case.

The design for this glasses case was made up while stitching, working from the center out. Combinations of Old Florentine and Hungarian Ground form the basis of the pattern. Carol Rome.

*Using the Binding Stitch:*

1. Turn under the canvas margins, trimming the excess to ½″ and mitering the corners. Press flat.

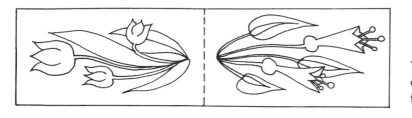

The bottoms of the front and back designs should face the center fold.

2. Fold the case in half, matching the top edges at either side. Using the binding stitch, stitch together both sides from the outer edge down to the fold. Then bind along the top edge, overlapping the last few stitches.

3. Make a lining of moiré silk or other slippery fabric seamed on both sides and folded at the bottom. Insert the lining into the case so that wrong sides are together. Turn under the top edge of the lining and blindstitch the lining to the lip of the case.

*Using a Sewing Machine:*

1. Tack cording to the needlepoint piece on the right side along the seamline. Go from center fold up one side, along the outer edge and back along the other side to the center fold. Also cord the top edge of the opposite side. Clip the cording at the corners.

2. Cut a lining (moiré silk is good) and lay it on the needlepoint piece, right sides facing.

3. Sew through all thicknesses on the seamline around 3 sides. Leave part of 1 corded section open for turning. Trim the excess to ½″ and clip the corners. Turn right side out and press flat.

4. Blindstitch the fourth side closed.

5. Fold the case in half. Hand-stitch the sides together using a curved needle and invisible nylon thread proceeding from edge to fold on each side.

## Lipstick Case

A lipstick case can be made for two or more lipsticks. These measurements are for a case that holds three 3″ lipsticks, allowing for a fold-over top and a little fullness at the bottom. When designing your case, keep in mind that there will be folds at the top and bottom. Orient the design vertically so that the fold-over top section matches the front design. Lipstick cases are set up, worked and finished according to the instructions for glasses cases. Sew on a snap closure after mounting.

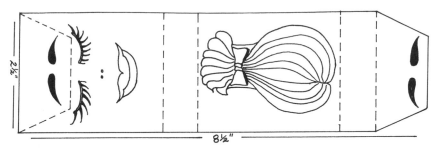

This drawing shows the direction to orient the design elements for front, back, and flap.

## Rain Hat Case

When planning a design for your rain hat case, orient the pattern so the motifs meet head-on at the edges. Finish according to the instructions for glasses cases.

The bottoms of the front and back designs should face the center fold.

## Scissors Case

A scissors case is an attractive, safe way to store your small pointed scissors. You may want to plan a design that picks up a pattern in the fabric of your yarn caddy. The best way to make the case is to use a 1-piece pattern. The canvas is folded across at the center, and the case is finished out according to the instructions for glasses cases.

When finished, the case will be on the bias, and you will want to account for this when planning the design. If you work with the grain of the canvas, the design will come out crooked on the finished piece. After finishing the case, stuff a piece of cork or a wad of Dacron in the tip to keep the points of the scissors from poking through.

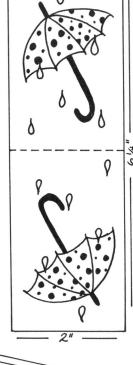

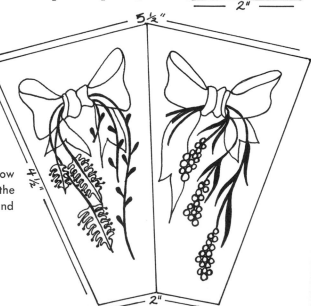

The design for a scissors case may look crooked now with the canvas opened out. However, when the piece is mounted the design will be oriented up and down but off the true canvas grain.

The totebag on the left was professionally mounted on leather. Tent stitch is used with accents of such stitches as Parisian and Chain. Mrs. Harold Sampson, Milwaukee, designed by Subo. Mrs. George C. French, Jr., of Milwaukee wrapped her sampler around a ready-made bag using Velcro strips as closures. In rows from left to right, you will recognize Shell, Milanese, Diamond Eyelet, a Herringbone variation, Fern, Oblique Slav, Triangle, Double, Leaf, "French Tramé," Herringbone Gone Wrong, Herringbone Couching, Tent with overstitching, Interwoven Herringbone, Herringbone, French, Rococo, Diamonds, Triple Leviathan (not shown in this book), and Smyrna.

There are many styles of handbags from which to choose, such as a fold-over clutch (good for evening wear), a totebag or a more formal, traditional purse that is mounted on a frame. First determine the kind of bag you want to make.

Make a paper pattern, taking the dimensions from a similar ready-made bag. Note carefully all gussets, pleats and folds. The fewer seams there are the better for mounting. If you are using hardware such as a frame handle, be sure to buy it beforehand. Check to see that the pattern fits the hardware properly.

Allow an extra ¼" stitching room plus the usual 1½" blank margins on all sides. Trace the pattern outlines on canvas and make sure the design is oriented so it will be right side up when the pieces are mounted. Avoid designs with pronounced vertical lines or stripes as these may become distorted in the finishing process. Tape or hem the canvas edges. Work the piece and block as usual.

Any handbag such as an evening fold-over clutch or totebag can be made up at home. However, purses that require complex frames and other hard-

Katharine G. Crain of Houston made a "mini-sampler" in bright orange, green, pink, and yellow for this purse using Byzantine, Oblong with Back-stitch, Leaf, and a Hungarian Ground variation with a Brick background. There are four more squares on the other side using different stitches. The purse was professionally mounted on orange vinyl.

ware should be mounted professionally. For home finishing, follow these steps:

1. Apply 1 or 2 layers of press-on Pellon to the back of the work to give it extra body and firmness. Trim off the excess margins to ½". Miter the corners and clip any curves.

2. If the purse has gussets or side panels, carefully match these up to the adjoining pieces, lining up mesh to mesh. Sew these edges together or join them with the binding stitch, going from the top to the bottom on each side and then across the bottom section if there is a seam there.

3. Cord and/or seam the top edge or finish it with the binding stitch.

4. A piece of heavy poster board cut to the same size as the bottom and inserted in the bottom gives the bag added support.

5. Make a lining insert out of heavy cotton, linen or plastic (a silk lining can be used for clutch bags). Make the lining about ⅓" larger all around than the purse dimensions. Blindstitch the lining into place matching the wrong side of the lining to the wrong side of the purse.

6. Handles and snaps or other closures can be added. Vinyl handles are recommended for totebags instead of needlepoint, braid or fabric ones, as these tend to soil with usage.

## 4
## HANDBAG INSERTS

A ready-made basket purse can be enhanced by adding an insert. Georgia Devlin's flower design is done in Tent with accents of Diagonal Mosaic (the large flower) and Mosaic. The binding stitch was used to finish the edges, and then the insert was glued in place on the basket.

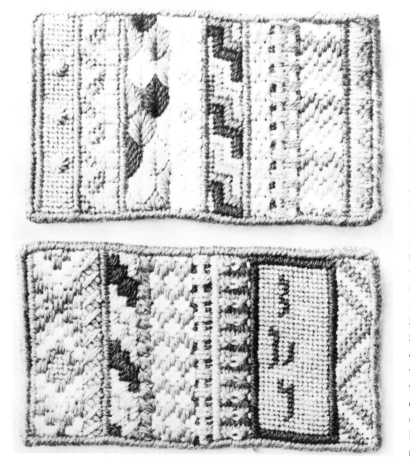

Front and back striped sampler inserts are ready to be glued to a small basket purse. From left to right, the stitches used are Tent with Ribbed Spiders, Diagonal Mosaic, Flat, Leaf, Hungarian, Byzantine, Oblong with Backstitch, Old Florentine (worked sideways), a Florentine pattern, and a Triangle variation. On the second panel, a Florentine pattern, Large Cross—Straight Cross, Diagonal Scotch, Italian Cross, Hungarian Ground, Old Florentine (sideways), Shell variation, a monogram in Tent, and Diagonal Mosaic are used. Gobelin Droit or Oblique is used to separate the rows. Georgia Devlin.

Make an insert for a ready-made purse or basket for added decoration.

Measure the area you want the insert to cover and mark the dimensions on tracing paper. Center the design in the tracing. Transfer the design to canvas that is cut with the usual 1½″ blank margins on all 4 sides. Tape or hem the canvas edges. Stitch the design and block.

1.  Turn under the worked edges. Trim the excess margin to ½″ and miter the corners. Press flat and hammer the corners if necessary.

2.  Finish the edges with the binding stitch and glue the insert to the purse. Or glue the insert down first and then glue braid trim over the unworked edges.

3.  You can make interchangeable inserts for a nice purse if you use Velcro strips for attaching the inserts. The bottom strips are glued to the purse, and the top strips are sewn to the wrong side of the insert.

# 5
# POCKETS

Family crests, school seals, monograms or company emblems all are good design motifs for pockets. The pocket should be worked on 14 count canvas or finer for best results.

Make a paper pattern of the pocket you want using a sewing pattern or a tracing from another garment as a guide. If you plan to use cording, allow an extra 3 or 4 rows of stitching all around for the finishing process. Don't forget to include 1½″ blank margin allowance when cutting the canvas. Hem or tape the canvas edges. Transfer the design to canvas. Stitch and block the piece as usual.

1.  Trim the excess canvas to ½″. Turn under the raw edges, being sure to miter corners and clip curves. Press the edges flat, hammering them if necessary. If no cording is used, bind stitch the edges. Attach a lining to the wrong side of the pocket with a handsewn blindstitch. Then tack the lined pocket to the garment itself.

2.  If cording is used, baste the cording along the seamline on the right side of the needlepoint. Lay a precut lining face down on top. Sew through all thicknesses with a machine around 3 sides. Trim the excess to ½″. Miter the corners and clip curves. Turn the piece right side out and blindstitch the fourth side closed. Tack the pocket to the garment.

# 6
# SLIPPERS

Slippers can be made with or without a back, although the backless ones (slides) have the advantage of less error in fitting. Scuffs and sandals are attractive when worked in needlepoint. In this case, one or more bands of stitchery go over the top of the foot and are mounted to leather soles.

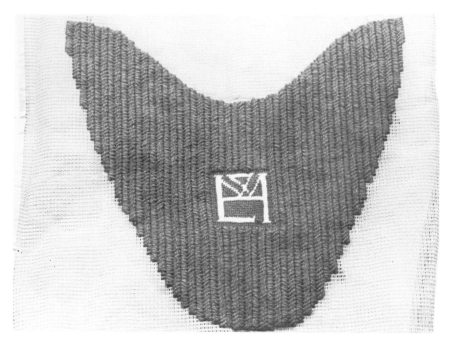

This is one of a pair of men's slippers worked on 10 count Penelope canvas. The monogram is worked in Diagonal Tent over 20 count, and the background is worked in full-size Stem. Carol Rome.

The use of 10 count canvas or finer is recommended for slippers. If you are making a representational design or a monogram, the design should face away from the person wearing the slipper or toward the toe. Make a paper pattern allowing the usual 1½″ blank margins all around. Tape or hem the canvas edges. Stitch and block.

Slippers should be professionally mounted. They are nicest when lined with leather. Check with a local shoe hospital for patterns and estimates on mounting before you begin the project.

# 7

# TENNIS RACQUET COVERS

There are many different racquet head shapes available today, which means that covers are not necessarily interchangeable. Use a plastic or cloth cover that fits *your* racquet as a guide for a pattern. Add ¼″ to ½″ extra stitching room and the usual 1½″ blank margins all around. Tape or hem the canvas edges. Any canvas gauge, including a size as large as 5 count, is effective for this project.

Mrs. Clifford Randall of Milwaukee worked this tennis racquet cover in Diagonal Tent for her daughter, Judy Thompson. Note the proper styling and size of the monogram in relation to the overall pattern. Designed by Designs for You.

Apply the design and stitch the piece. When finished, the racquet cover must be subjected to very careful blocking.

It is not recommended that you attempt to mount a tennis racquet cover at home unless you are an expert on a sewing machine, as there are sharp curves, boxing, cording and a zipper to contend with. Be sure to get a firm estimate on finishing before starting the project. Generally, sailcloth or lightweight vinyl is used for the backing and cording. A lining of some kind should be included to prevent the back of the needlepoint from snagging on the racquet. A zipper is inserted up one side.

# 8
# VESTS

A vest can be made in 1 or 3 pieces. You will find many suitable patterns in sewing catalogs, or you can use a vest you already have as a pattern guide. A vest with simple, straight lines will make up much more easily than one with curves and darts. The use of canvas larger than 10 count is not recommended, as the finished garment would be too heavy to wear.

Mrs. Lonnie P. Mann of St. Louis chose the personal interests and hobbies of her son, who is a doctor of veterinary medicine, as a design theme for this lovely traditional vest worked in Tent. Gold horseshoe buttons add an elegant finishing touch to her gift.

Be sure the pattern fits properly, especially if you are planning a man's vest; any necessary alterations should be made beforehand. If you are planning to use hooks and eyes or buttons for fastenings, allow for overlapping at the center front when working out your design or you may lose part of the pattern when the vest is mounted.

Cut the canvas with the usual 1½" blank margins plus ½" extra stitching room on each side for ease and seams. Tape or hem the canvas edges. Transfer the design. Work and block the piece(s).

*Using a Sewing Machine:*

1. Apply press-on Pellon to the wrong side of the needlepoint to keep it from crawling out of shape if needed.

2. Cording is optional. If you are using cording, baste it along the seam line on the right side of the needlepoint at the center front, neck, armholes and hem.

3. A light, slippery fabric is recommended for the lining. The shoulder seams of the lining and the needlepoint vest should be sewn separately by machine.

This drawing illustrates how a vest can be laid out on canvas in three separate pieces or as a single unit. Most men's vests have needlepointed fronts only.

4. Place the lining on the needlepoint, right sides together. Machine-stitch all seams except the side seams (and hem) using a ⅝" seam allowance that includes 1 or 2 worked rows.

5. Open out the vest and lining. Machine-stitch the side seams. Clip the curves and trim the excess to ½".

6. Blindstitch the hem closed. Press flat and add closures if desired.

*Using the Binding Stitch:*

If you prefer, the center front, neck, armholes and hem can be finished with the binding stitch. Then a precut, machine-stitched lining is blind-stitched to the wrong side of the vest.

Men's vests are quite complicated to make up and require some tailoring. If you are going to have this done professionally, make sure to get a firm quote before starting the project. This can be *very* expensive.

## 9
## BELLPULLS

## HOUSEHOLD FURNISHINGS

Bellpulls, which were functional items in our grandparents' homes, today are used as a decorative touch. They can be any length and width; however, 54" x 6" is a popular size. Purchase the hardware before starting the project. If you prefer, you can use dowel rods, wooden rings or braid and tassels instead of expensive hardware. Decide in advance.

The needlepoint bellpull should be ½" narrower than the inside measurement of the shank of the hardware. After determining the length, width and design, cut the canvas with the usual 1½" blank margins. Be sure to straighten the canvas if it is distorted from being rolled. Tape or hem the canvas edges. Stitch and block the piece.

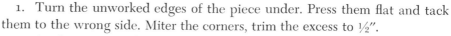

1. Turn the unworked edges of the piece under. Press them flat and tack them to the wrong side. Miter the corners, trim the excess to ½″.

2. Apply a piece of press-on Pellon to the reverse side of the piece to keep it from crawling out of shape and losing body.

3. If you want to use cording, tack it on by hand on each edge along the back of the piece.

4. Hand blindstitch a moiré silk backing to the wrong side and attach the hardware.

Machine finishing is not very successful for bellpulls. However, you may want to use the binding stitch to finish the edges before adding the backing.

This early American bellpull is worked in rows of narrow, oblong crosses. Corresponding colors of Backstitching are worked between the rows. A stepped rainbow effect is created by shading. *Courtesy of the Historic Deerfield Collection, Deerfield, Massachusetts.*

# 10

# BOOK JACKETS, CHECKBOOK AND TELEPHONE BOOK COVERS

In planning a design for a book jacket, try to determine in advance where the book will be kept. Telephone books and other books with hand-worked jackets often will be placed on a flat surface for display so the back cover won't show. In this case, you may decide to work the front section only.

Remember when planning a checkbook cover that the canvas will be folded across the top. Therefore, the design motifs should meet head-on at the fold. Small book covers and checkbook covers should be worked on 14 count canvas or finer for best results. Telephone book covers can be worked on any gauge canvas.

Measure the length and width of the book you are planning to cover. Trace the outline on paper, adding ¼″ extra stitching room to each edge plus the usual 1½″ margins. Tape or hem the canvas edges. Stitch and block the piece and use a sewing machine to finish the book cover.

Mrs. Cora Montgomery Goss of Denver added highlights to her bird design in Tent stitch by working some areas with cotton embroidery floss. A silk lining was used to finish the book jacket.

This detail of a Haggadah cover by Mrs. Benjamin Paley of Houston illustrates the effective use of metal thread stitching. The design is worked in Diagonal Tent; the background (outside this picture) is worked in Gobelin Droit.

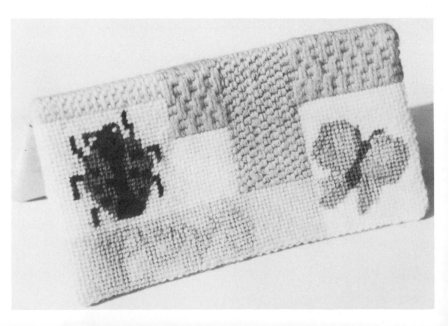

Needle Nuts designed this attractive checkbook cover for Lé Stitcherie, Houston. Parisian, Old Florentine, and Double Brick add texture to the design.

If you are planning to needlepoint both sides of a book jacket, remember that the front cover is on the right side.

The front and back designs for a checkbook cover should meet head on at the center fold.

    1. Baste cording to the right side of the needlepoint piece, if you are planning to use cording. (Cording should not be used on checkbook covers because it adds too much bulk.)

    2. Cut the lining piece and 2 pieces of the same fabric for the pockets that will hold the jacket on the book. Each of the 2 pocket pieces will be folded in half.

    3. Place the 2 pockets at the side edges on the right side of the needle-

point piece with the folds facing the center. Place the lining right side down on top of the pockets and needlepoint.

4. Sew through all thicknesses of this sandwich twice on 3 sides. Miter the corners and trim the excess to ½″. Press flat and hammer the corners if necessary. Turn right side out. Turn under the raw edges and blindstitch the fourth side closed. Press flat.

5. Insert the book with front and back bindings slipped into the pockets.

*Notes on Telephone Book Covers:* A telephone book cover should have an interlining of heavy poster board scored at the folding places to keep the book from flopping around. This can be slipped into the pockets before the book is inserted. This method of mounting a telephone book cover is less expensive than a leather binding and can be done at home. The cover can be removed for cleaning. However, you may want the cover to be professionally mounted. If so, get a firm quote before starting the project.

*Notes on Inserts:* An easy and very effective way to make a special book cover is to buy a ready-made cover for a telephone book, address book, or whatever, and then make an insert. This piece can be finished out according to the instructions for handbag inserts.

# 11

## BRICK DOORSTOP COVERS

Before making a doorstop cover, carefully measure the brick you plan to use, determining the overall length and width as well as the height and top area. Mark the dimensions on the canvas, adding ⅛″ extra stitching room all around for ease plus the usual 1½″ blank margins. Be sure to include the top dimensions on the canvas so you can properly center the design. Hem or tape the canvas edges. Stitch and block the piece.

1. Sew the corner edges together by machine from the wrong side. Or use the binding stitch to join the corners starting from the bottom edges and working toward the top of the cover. Trim the excess to ½″.

2. Pad the brick with layers of Dacron batting and slip the needlepoint cover over the brick.

The side designs on a brick doorstop cover should face toward the middle so they will come out right side up when the piece is mounted.

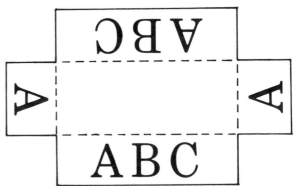

Crewel and tapestry yarns went into this brick doorstop cover, which is ready for mounting. From the center out, you will recognize Tent with overlaid stitches, a Florentine pattern, Parisian, Mosaic, Brick, Star, a Flat variation, Gobelin Droit, Cashmere, Crossed Corners, Smyrna, Interlocking Gobelin, Flat, and Knotted. Mrs. Alan W. Moore, Des Moines.

3. Fold the unworked edges to the underside of the brick and lace them tight with long zigzag stitches from end to end and side to side using heavy-duty thread. Or use the binding stitch to finish the bottom edges and then lace.

4. Glue felt to the bottom of the brick.

The Tent stitch turtle hatchling is going toward a "Florentine Sea" on this paperweight worked over 16 count canvas. The reverse side of the piece is worked too, and there is a verse around the four sides. Mary Cooke Woodward, Washington, D.C.

*Notes on Paperweights:* Any uniformly shaped, heavy object can be used inside. Measure the weighting object carefully and add ⅛″ stitching room plus the usual 1½″ blank margins to these dimensions. Use 14 count canvas or finer and finish according to the above instructions.

## 12
## CHAIR, BENCH AND FOOTSTOOL SEATS

Canvas embroidery has been used for centuries as upholstery for many different styles and pieces of furniture. It makes a highly decorative, long-wearing surface and is an attractive addition to the decor of any room.

Mrs. James A. Kilgroe of Denver has started a set of six chairs with different, related designs. The themes here are the pumpkin and the pomegranate. The design areas are worked in Tent, and Jacquard is used for the backgrounds.

In working a set of chair seats, do not forego the challenge of working each piece in a different, but related design. This makes the work more exciting, and the finished set will be made up of a harmonious group of unique pieces.

This beautiful pastel shaded piano bench cover was worked by Mrs. E. J. Hoffer of Houston and designed by Pat Sampson. The large flowers are worked in Split Gobelin with Turkey Tufting centers and Diagonal Mosaic with French Knot centers. The butterflies are worked in Tent, and the small flowers are worked in French and Double Brick. The background is worked in Gobelin Droit.

The most important step in preparing a seat project is the initial measuring. Determine the exact dimensions by measuring from front to back and from side to side at the *widest* points. To these dimensions add 2″ to be worked on each side. This may seem like a lot of extra stitching. However, half this work will be taken up in fullness and ease, and the other half is needed for pulling under during the finishing process.

If the piece has a very irregular shape, make a pattern directly from it. Again, enlarge this tracing 2″ all around and mark the canvas accordingly. Add the usual 1½″ blank margins and hem or tape the canvas edges.

It is recommended that you have an upholsterer mount the finished piece on the chair, bench or footstool you have selected. Get a firm quote on the charges beforehand and decide whether you want cording, braid or gimp tacks to finish the piece out. Request that the piece be Scotch-garded for protection against spills and soiling.

It is a good idea to give the upholsterer several lengths of leftover yarn to tuck under the worked piece inside the mounting in case repairs are ever necessary in the future. The foresightedness of many embroiderers has saved museum curatorial staffs from the difficult task of matching yarn when repairing heritage pieces!

A set of coasters is an excellent project for children to work since the areas to be stitched are small and manageable. A popular size for coasters is 3½″ x 3½″. However, they can be made with different dimensions. A set of 4 coasters is nice, with the designs related but not exactly the same. Popular motifs are animals, fruits, vegetables or flowers.

To economize, work all 4 coasters on 1 strip of canvas. When marking the design off on the canvas, allow the usual 1½″ blank margins on all sides. This will mean that you should allow approximately 3″ between each coaster. Tape or hem the canvas edges. Stitch the coasters. Cut the coasters apart and block them separately.

1. Fold under the unworked margins, trimming the excess to ½″ and mitering the corners to eliminate bulk. Press the margins flat against the wrong side of the needlepoint.

2. Glue the piece directly to poster board precut to the coaster measurements. Or use the binding stitch to finish the edges before the poster board is glued in place.

3. Glue a piece of cork or felt to the bottom of the sandwich and put the coasters between heavy books to dry.

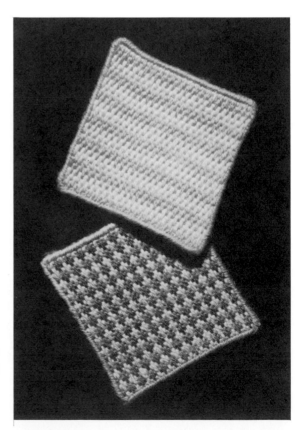

Hungarian and 4 count Brick make up these coasters, which were finished with the binding stitch. Georgia Devlin.

# DIRECTOR'S CHAIRS

Gay colors and bold designs are the hallmark of these director's chairs at Lé Stitcherie, designed by Needle Nuts. The first chair is worked in a patchwork of "trompe l'oeil" (fool-the-eye) wild animal skin patterns in Tent stitch. The second chair, again worked in Tent, has a bright patchwork pattern where color creates the interest. Old Florentine and Brick are added to Tent to create texture in the third and fourth chairs. Note the simplicity and elegance of the simple chrome frames.

Director's chairs are available with sailcloth, leather or vinyl backs and slings. The chair frames come in chrome or wood. Use the original chair covers as a pattern guide, allowing the usual 1½" blank margins on all sides and an extra ½" stitching room for ease. Any gauge canvas is effective for this project. However, since there is a large area to stitch, you may prefer to use 12 count or larger.

Cut 1 long strip of canvas to make the back section. Later, this will be joined together in a continuous tube. The seam should *not* fall in the center back where it is conspicuous, but right up next to one of the uprights that support the back section. Therefore, notice where the center of the design should fall on the back section when planning the design and marking the canvas. Cut a separate piece for the seat section. Tape or hem the canvas edges and stitch and block as usual.

*Back Section:*

1. If you plan to use cording, machine-stitch it along the seamline on the right side of the needlepoint along half the length of the back section on the top and bottom edges.

2. Pin sections of sailcloth lining where the two uprights fit through. Turn under the top and bottom hems and blindstitch the lining pieces in place.

3. Seam the back section together into a tube by machine or by one of the canvas joining methods.

4. Blindstitch the top and bottom edges together or use the binding stitch. Leave open enough room for the frame uprights. Slip the new cover over the uprights.

*Seat:*

1. Baste cording along the seamline on the right side of the needlepoint

seat section. Machine-stitch 2 layers of sailcloth to the needlepoint piece, right sides together, leaving open enough room to reverse the piece. Clip the corners and trim the excess to ½″. Turn the sling right side out and blindstitch the opening closed. Press flat.

2. Fold back the ends of the sling and sew the piece to itself around the two seat frame supports for chrome chairs. If you are using a wood-framed director's chair, the ends of the new sling will have to be forced into the grooves under the arm sections.

3. The seat section can be finished out as a cushion to be used on top of the original sling according to the instructions for boxed pillows if preferred.

4. Scotch-gard both sections.

## 15
## LUGGAGE RACK STRAPS

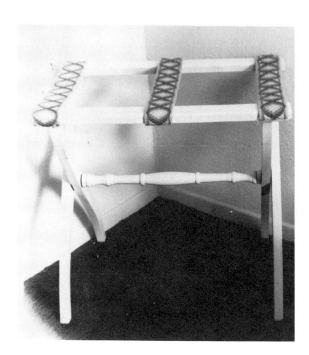

A luggage rack is a nice accessory for a guest room. This one is worked in a Florentine pattern in colors that match the wallpaper and bed quilt. Carol Rome.

Most luggage racks have two or three straps that can serve as a pattern guide. To determine the proper length, measure across the open rack, allowing 2″ extra stitching on each end for mounting the straps to the rack. The width is optional. Add the usual 1½″ blank margins all around when marking the canvas and orient the design vertically. Tape or hem the canvas edges. Stitch and block the piece as usual.

Follow steps 1 through 4 for finishing a bellpull. The finished straps can be tacked or stapled right on top of the original ones on the underside of the rack. If you are planning to paint the rack, remember to do this *before* adding the new straps.

The mirror frame can be adapted to serve as a picture mat. Here, nursery rhyme characters in Diagonal Tent surround a photograph of the family's youngest members. Mrs. W. A. Camp, Houston, designed by Designs for You.

Virginia D. Crain of Houston worked this mirror frame on 10 count canvas. She used the Leaf stitch in blue, green, and yellow to create a very attractive, simple frame.

When planning a mirror frame, make sure the dimensions and design enhance the surrounded mirror. Trace the measurements including the center area, which will be removed later, onto canvas. Allow ⅛″ extra stitching room on both the inside and outside edges for ease plus the usual 1½″ margins on the 4 outside edges. Tape or hem the canvas edges. Transfer the design to canvas. Stitch and block the piece.

1. Apply tabs of press-on Pellon at the center corners for reinforcement. Cut open the center in an X right up to the stitched edges. (You may want to leave the last row or 2 next to the center opening unstitched. If the design is painted on the canvas, the tiny area of unworked canvas will not show when it is turned under.) Trim some of the excess.

2. Cut a piece of thin plywood or a triple thickness of stiff poster board to the dimensions of the stitching minus the ⅛″ ease allowance. Fold the center unworked margins back over the plywood or poster board. Glue down. Miter the outside corners and turn the outside edges back over the plywood or poster board. Glue down and put the piece between heavy books to dry.

3. Fix a mirror to the wrong side of the frame using adhesive or other strong, sticky tape. Add hardware to a strip of wood glued to the back of the mirror.

A mat for a picture can be made according to these instructions using a layer of poster board. A ready-made frame is placed over the picture and mat.

A tiny easel is an attractive way to display a needlepoint picture. Mrs. William Fowles of Des Moines has used Tent to work this poppy design. Note how the flowers are broken down into several color areas to create realistic modeling. Designed by Clara Waever.

Mrs. Philip Kuehn, Jr., of Grafton, Wisc., stitched this lovely house portrait as a gift for Mr. and Mrs. David Uihlein, whose initials appear below their house. The sky and grass are worked in Diagonal Tent. The house roof is Old Florentine, and the section at the right of the house is Bokhara Couching. From left to right, the trees behind the house are worked in Hungarian, Diamond Eyelet, Brick, Mosaic, Gobelin Oblique, Gobelin Oblique (again), Herringbone Gone Wrong, Leaf, and Rosettes. The design is well balanced and well proportioned for the space it occupies. No one could mistake this piece for a painting despite its fine detail because of the excellent textured effects produced by the judicious use of a combination of canvas stitches.

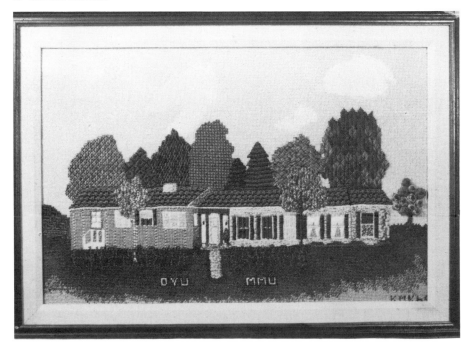

Pictures can be any size or shape. They can be framed and used on tiny easels or hung on the wall. Traditional mats do not particularly enhance the look of the finished piece. A more effective treatment is an added border of decorative stitches. Many people prefer to frame the picture without glass so the texture of the stitches is readily available to the eye and the touch.

The needlepoint piece should be ⅛″ smaller than the frame you select. Heavy poster board or cardboard for small pictures and ¼″ plywood for larger pictures make good backing materials. The backing piece should be made ⅛″ smaller than the frame. If you prefer, a wooden frame stretcher can be used instead of a backing; however, it is more expensive.

Add 1½″ blank margins on all sides of the design. Hem or tape the cut canvas edges. Stitch and block the piece as usual.

1. Fold the unworked margins of the needlepoint piece over the poster board or plywood, mitering the corners and trimming the excess. These edges can be glued or tacked down, or they can be "laced" from side to side and end to end across the backing material with heavy-duty thread. Tack or glue down the fold at the corners.

2. Insert the piece into the frame. Finish off the back with brown paper and the necessary hardware.

This Mediterranean scene is worked entirely in 4 count Brick, with some sections worked vertically and others horizontally. The "cobbled" effect of this stitch adds interest to the design. Mrs. John C. Stears, Denver, designed by Wm. Briggs & Co., Ltd.

Mrs. Herman Merker of Milwaukee used a variety of canvas stitches to work the Camelot crest. The background is Gobelin Droit. Note the use of an uneven count Gobelin Droit below the tree to fill in an area with curves. The tree trunk is in Cross stitch. The crest is made up of Gobelin Droit, Old Florentine, Tent, and Brick, and the rest of the design is in Tent. Designed by Subo.

# 18
# PILLOWS

Pillows probably are the most popular needlepoint project to do, and they come in an endless array of sizes and shapes. Any canvas gauge can be used for pillows. Determine the dimensions you want and transfer the measurements to tracing paper. Center the design and mark the design and outlines on canvas, adding the usual 1½″ blank margins all around. Tape or hem the canvas edges and stitch the piece. Block as usual.

Keep the following options in mind when deciding how you want the finished pillow to look. It can be finished with a knife edge, or it can be boxed. Cording, fringe or tassels add a decorative touch. The choices you make should enhance the needlepoint piece in color, weight and texture. Note: round pillows always should be boxed and corded or the edges will tend to ripple unattractively.

Pillows, pillows! Combinations of stitches and bright colors create attractive designs. Designed by Subo. Mrs. Eugene Kerns of Milwaukee worked the eagle pillow. Stripes of Gobelin Droit and Brick make up the background. The eagle's head and wing tops are worked in Oblique Slav, and Split Gobelin is used on the wings. The shield is worked in Tent, and Chain is used for outlining. Mrs. Harold Sampson of Milwaukee worked the abstract flower pillow below the eagle. Brick and Split Gobelin with Tent outlines make up the flower, and Star is used in the border. Lolita Friedlen of Milwaukee used Diagonal Scotch, Diagonal Mosaic, Tent, Mosaic, French Knots, and Brick in her mod flower sampler. The tulip flowers are worked in Brick, Crossed Corners, Cashmere, and Mosaic. The leaves and background of this pillow are worked in Tent. Mrs. Harry Wilkins, Milwaukee.

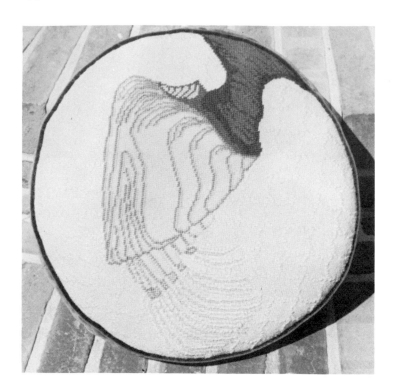

The inspiration for this design came from an old engraving of a sea barnacle. The scallops simulating the sea current are worked in uneven count Tent stitches. Mary Cooke Woodward, Washington, D.C.

If you are using cording or fringe, make it beforehand. The gauge of cording you use should be fine for small pillows and medium to thick for larger ones. The length of cording is the distance around the needlepoint piece plus a 1″ seam allowance. Boxed pillows have cording on both sides of the boxing, so make a double amount of cording.

*Knife-edged Pillows:*

1. Trim the blank canvas to ½″. Cut the backing fabric the same size and cut the corners of both canvas and fabric to a taper to avoid a dog-eared look. Prepare fringe, tassels or fabric cording.

2. Pin cording or fringe to the right side of the needlepoint piece along the seamline. (Pin tassels on the right side of the piece at the corners.) Baste the cording in place, being sure to clip the cording at the corners and on any curves.

3. Lay the needlepoint piece down on the backing piece, right sides together. Stitch by machine through all thicknesses, following the cording stitches around 3 sides of the pillow. Restitch a second time for added strength.

4. Trim the corners and excess margins and clip curves. Reverse the pillow so it is right side out.

5. Stuff the pillow with down, kapok or Dacron batting or use a ready-made muslin pillow that is 1″ larger than the outer cover. Shredded foam

rubber can be used as a stuffer; however, it tends to stick to things, making a mess unless you are very careful.

6. Blindstitch the fourth side closed.

*Boxed Pillows:*

1. Trim the blank canvas and taper the corners of the canvas. Cut the fabric for boxings. Most boxings are 1½″ to 2″ wide when finished. Allow a ½″ seam allowance on either side, so cut a fabric strip 2½″ to 3″ wide. The length should be the distance around the piece plus an extra 1″ for seam allowance.

2. Baste cording or fringe to the right sides of the needlepoint piece and the backing piece on the seam line.

3. Lay the needlepoint piece down on the boxing strip, right sides together. The boxing strip seam should be located at the middle of one of the sides of the needlepoint piece. Stitch along on top of the cording stitches all the way around the piece, being sure to clip the boxing at the corners. Restitch this seam for added strength.

4. Sew the 2 edges of the boxing together where they meet, using a ½″ seam.

5. Place the backing piece on the boxing strip, right sides together (and facing the right side of the needlepoint piece). Stitch twice around 3 sides, following the cording stitches and clipping the boxing at the corners.

6. Follow steps 4 through 6 for knife-edged pillows for the rest of the finishing process.

*Notes on the Binding Stitch:* If you have needlepointed both sides of a pillow, you can finish it very simply by joining the edges of the 4 sides together with the binding stitch. Stuff the pillow before the last side is bound closed or insert a ready-made pillow.

# 19
# PILLOW INSERTS

Pillow inserts are framed in the middle of fabric- or leather-covered pillows. Cording or braid usually is sewn along the edges of the turned-under needlepoint to give the piece a finished look.

The size of the insert is a matter of personal choice. However, the pillow should be at least 2″ wider all around for an uncrowded appearance. The finished piece should be at least 10″, especially when it will be knife-edged, or you will end up with an "overgrown pincushion" that looks rather silly.

Allow the usual 1½″ blank margins on all sides when cutting the canvas. Tape or hem the canvas edges. Then stitch and block the piece.

1. Trim the excess canvas to ½″, miter the corners. Machine-stitch cording along the seamline on the right side of the needlepoint, clipping the cording at the corners.

Karen Kirkpatrick of Houston added interest to this mushroom pillow insert by using a combination of canvas stitches. Designed by Merribee. The background uses a combination of Double and Single Brick, the big mushroom is in Herringbone, and the small mushroom is in Leaf. Tent and Gobelin Droit variations are also used in small sections of the design.

2. Turn under the excess canvas and raw cording edges and press flat.

3. Before assembling the pillow, machine-baste the insert in place on the right side of the front fabric through the insert and fabric one row inside the worked area or through the cording stitching. This stitching will not show since the cording will have a tendency to roll over it. This method of applying the insert is stronger than hand-sewing the piece to the front of the pillow.

4. Assemble the pillow according to the instructions for pillows.

*Notes:* Braid laid over the insert edges can be used instead of cording. Hand-whip this on after the insert is secured to the front fabric. If you are using a ready-made pillow, unzip and remove the cover for ease in handling. Proceed as above. The binding stitch also can be used to finish the edges of the insert before it is sewn to the pillow front.

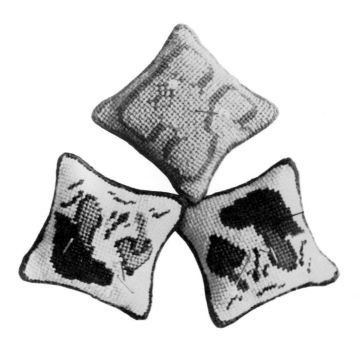

Three young children of Houston needlepointers worked these tiny pincushions in Tent stitch. Lara Leigh Gardere, age eleven; Cathy Stillwell, age ten; and Alyson Crouch, age nine.

Pincushions are actually miniature pillows and are finished just as you would finish a pillow. Popular sizes for knife-edged pincushions are 5″ x 5″ or 6″ x 6″. Rectangular, round or odd-shaped ones also can be done in approximately the same sizes. Remember to cut the canvas with a 1½″ blank margin on each side. Tape or hem the canvas edges.

Pincushions can be worked on both sides or on one side using a fabric backing. They can be corded, fringed, or the edges can be joined with the binding stitch. Stuff the finished pincushion with old stockings or regular pillow stuffing.

Because this is a small project, 14 count canvas or finer should be used as well as small gauge cording and a relatively simple design. A pincushion makes an excellent baby gift and is a project that can be worked easily by children.

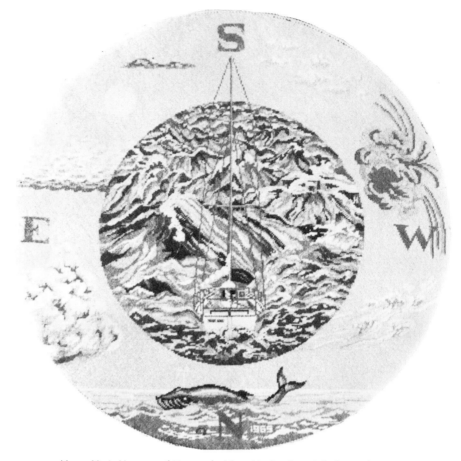

Mary H. J. Harper of Katonah, New York, chronicled a sailing trip she and her husband made to Bermuda on their 33-foot cutter. Mili Holmes helped Mrs. Harper plan the design, which records events that occurred and noteworthy sights. The design elements have been worked out so that there is good rhythm and movement within the circular space. The rug, later turned into a fire screen to protect it from the family cat, is stitched with Tent.

Rugs can be made in any width, length or shape. A 4′ x 5′ is a popular size for an accent rug or for use under coffee tables. Both Penelope and mono canvas are suitable for this kind of project in a gauge as fine as 10–12 count or as large as 3–5 count.

If you choose to do a fairly small rug, it usually can be worked in one piece. However, larger ones should be worked in several sections. Some people use frames to work large pieces, as they tend to be heavy and cumbersome.

Small or large, a rug is a major undertaking both in time and expense. You may want to start a rug and keep it going as a long-term project while working a series of smaller pieces. Avoid designs with large expanses of background or boredom is sure to set in, and you will be tempted to abandon the project in midstream.

Traditionally Diagonal Tent has been used on rugs. However, do not overlook some of the other canvas stitches for a project of this type. When selecting stitches for a rug, make sure they are fairly tight and snagproof and that they have a firm backing. Allow the usual 1½″ blank margins on each side of all sections when cutting the canvas. Hem or tape the canvas edges.

Blocking a finished rug requires a large area and strong muscles! Rugs worked in sections will have to be blocked twice, first with the pieces apart, then after they have been bound together. The rug must be thoroughly dry before mounting, and this can take two or three days.

1. A spray-on adhesive (such as Scotch Spra-Ment Adhesive) is applied to the back, and a piece of precut muslin is fixed to this. This stabilizing process will assure that the rug will retain its shape and body.

2. The raw edges are turned under and whipped to the wrong side of the rug using waxed linen rug thread. Be sure no needlepoint stitching is turned under at the edges or there will be extra bulk, and the rug will not lie flat.

3. Bind the edges with the binding stitch. Bind the side edges only if fringing is to be added.

4. If the rug is to be laid over a carpet, a lining of ducking is blindstitched to the wrong side. A burlap lining is used if the rug is going to be laid on a bare floor.

5. Fringe the ends if desired.

*Notes:* Rugs worked in sections will have to be joined by machine or the binding stitch before the piece can be mounted. Instructions for joining canvas are found on pages 215-220.

Six members of the Denver Cerebral Palsy Auxiliary worked this rug as a benefit prize in a workshop expansion project. Jacqueline Ambler used Colorado wildflowers as the theme for the rug design. The rug was worked in six sections.

This sampler is the result of Carol Rome's first attempt at needlepoint. The colors were chosen to match some of those in the living room oriental carpet. From left to right in rows, the stitches are Gobelin Droit, Hungarian Ground, Parisian, Mosaic, Brick, Split Gobelin, Small Chequer, a Florentine pattern worked sideways, Gobelin Oblique, Star, French, Hungarian, Oblong with Backstitch, Smyrna, Tent with Ribbed Spiders, Large Chequer, Old Florentine, Flat, Bokhara Couching, Byzantine, Triangle, Double, Diagonal Mosaic, Large Cross—Straight Cross, Herringbone, Moorish, Crossed Corners, Diamonds, Stem with Backstitch, Long-Armed Cross, Diamond Eyelet, Leaf (with two colors worked at the same time), Double Straight Cross, Diagonal Scotch, two-color Herringbone, monogram in Tent.

The following formula is an excellent way to set up a sampler. Use a piece of 14 count mono canvas. Mark off squares of 24 mesh with 6 mesh between each square. The number of squares you choose to do will determine the size and shape of the canvas piece needed. Generally, an 18″ x 18″ piece will be adequate for up to 36 squares (6 rows of 6 squares each). If you are doing less than 24 squares, a smaller piece of canvas can be used.

Remember to leave a 1½″ blank margin all around before cutting. Hem or tape the canvas edges. Use a pencil for marking the squares so you can erase miscounted lines. Spray the marked canvas with an art fixative to prevent smudging if necessary.

Sabina Maltz of Houston made these festive sampler pillows in bright colors and trimmed them with tassels and pompoms in matching yarn colors. Note the effective use of Gobelin Droit in alternating rows over a 3 count, then a 6 count on the middle pillow.

Georgia Devlin worked her round sampler in pastel colors. The left half of the design from top to bottom contains the following stitches: Large Chequer, a Tent butterfly surrounded by Stem, a Tent flower with Ribbed Spider center, Double Straight Cross, a Florentine pattern, Vandyke, and Hungarian variation. Herringbone, Hungarian Ground, Old Florentine, Leaf, Diagonal Scotch, a Tent monogram and date surrounded by Mosaic, a Tent ladybug surrounded by Brick, Milanese, and Italian Cross occupy the right half of the sampler.

This German sampler was worked in 1700 on coarse linen. Silk thread was used to stitch the piece; you will recognize Stem, Cross, Rococo, Crossed Corners, and Tent among other stitches. *Courtesy of the Cooper-Hewitt Museum of Design, Smithsonian Institution, New York.*

The background rows usually are reserved for practicing Diagonal Tent. Some people prefer to work this after the squares have been filled in, and others before. Either two color families with three shades in each or six unrelated colors make a beautiful sampler.

Many people use the finished piece for a pillow. The sampler also can be used for a totebag, a small bolster, a square stool top or book cover to name a few "destinations." Make a row-by-row listing of the stitches you have used for quick reference.

# 23
# WALL HANGINGS

Wall hangings can be designed in any size or shape and can be worked over any gauge mesh. They are treated like rugs in blocking and finishing. Scotch-garded cotton or moiré silk are good choices for backing.

After lining and mounting the wall hanging, loops of the backing fabric or small rings are sewn along the top edge at regular intervals for the hanging rod to slip through. Drapery weights should be sewn inside the mounting along the bottom edge, or a brass rod can be slipped between the worked piece and the backing at the bottom to make the piece hang straight. (The rod should be ½" shorter at each end than the width of the finished piece.)

Mrs. Thomas T. Richmond of New Canaan, Connecticut, used a variety of stitches to enhance the beauty of this prize-winning church antependium, designed by Mili Holmes. The background is worked in a combination of Gobelin Droit and Crossed Corners. The rays of the sunburst are in Moorish, Hungarian Ground variation, and Gobelin Droit. The crowns are in Tent, and the surrounding area is in Hungarian.

"Toy Cats" was made for her child's room by Lara Kline of Delmar, New York. Her design sources included children's books, and fanciful colors have gone into the hanging. Mrs. Kline broke up the background with arrangements of leaves, some of which were stitched by other members of the family. The piece is worked in Tent.

## OTHER PROJECT SUGGESTIONS

*Household Furnishings*
blotter ends
bookends
bookmarks
card table covers
Christmas ornaments
Christmas stockings
cornice boards
curtain tiebacks
headboards
hi-fi speaker covers
napkin rings
screens
tissue box covers
wastebasket covers

*Personal Accessories*
barrettes
credit card cases
dog collars
golf club covers
guitar straps
hair bands
key chains
neckbands
neckties
pins
wristwatch bands

Mrs. Harry Powell Wilson, Jr., of Denver designed and worked these lovely Christmas stockings for her children. The main designs were worked in Tent over 14 count canvas with Gobelin Oblique surrounding the names. Santa's face is worked on 18 count canvas, which Mrs. Wilson laid over the base piece, working through both layers. His beard is in Turkey Tufting.

Virginia D. Crain of Houston worked these Christmas stockings over 5 count canvas. Note the use of Turkey Tufting for the Santa beards. The Christmas tree skirt was worked in sections by members of Kappa Kappa Gamma in Houston as a benefit prize for a charitable function. The skirt was designed by Georgia Devlin and is owned by Dee Elder.

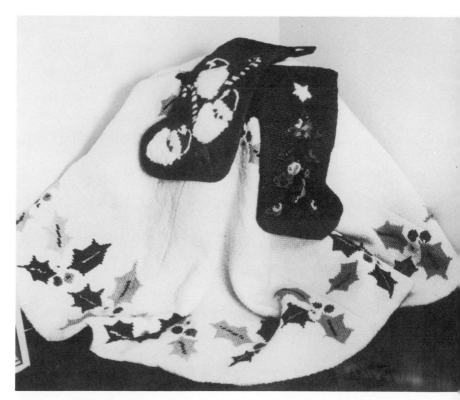

Mrs. P. Michael Wells of Houston added French Knots to these Christmas mini-pictures which are displayed at the holiday season on tiny easels. The same patterns could be used for coasters.

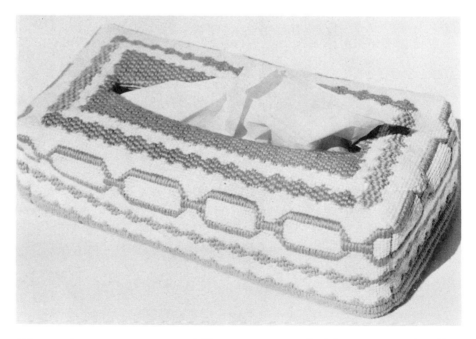

What a nice way to store tissue! This cover was worked by Betty Passel in Tent, Double Brick, and Gobelin Droit for Lé Stitcherie. Designed by Arlette.

Matching letter box and blotter ends were made with the family crest as the design theme by Mrs. Francis MeVay of East Williston, New York, designed by Rosetta Larsen. The pieces are worked over a fine gauge canvas in Tent stitch with wool and silk threads.

Teen-agers like neckbands and personalized key chains. These projects are quick to work up and make nice gifts. Lé Stitcherie.

Golf club covers make a gift both men and women golfers would appreciate. Karen Kirkpatrick of Houston worked this set in Tent stitch and had them professionally mounted.

Inserts for a sweater add an elegant touch. These floral strips are worked in Tent stitch in soft colors that blend nicely with the color of the sweater. Mary Peterson, Houston.

## MOUNTING RESOURCES

By and large, the needlework specialty shop where you buy canvas and yarn will have access to local resources that block and mount anything from a glasses case to a director's chair according to your specifications. The advantage of having your work mounted locally is that there usually is not a long waiting period. There are a few items that even the shops have to send off for mounting. The following are reputable companies to whom you can send your work for mounting if no local resources are available.

Modern Needlepoint Mounting Company
11 West 32nd Street
New York, N.Y. 10001
212–279–3263

(Specializing in all kinds of purses. Also, tennis racquet covers, book jackets, picture frames, bellpulls, and so on. Write for price list.)

The Spinning Wheel Shop
Mrs. W. A. Camp
903 Marshall
Houston, Texas 77006
713–524–6780

(Pillows, cases, director's chairs, rugs, and so on.)

L. B. Evans' Son Company
37 Water Street
Wakefield, Massachusetts 01880
617–245–9000
(Attention: Muriel Colson)

(Men's slippers bound and lined with leather. Write for paper patterns and costs.)

# CHAPTER 6

# Notes on Finishing

Cat pillow by Jean Kommel, Roslyn, N.Y. The beaded tassels enhance the look of this charming design.

# INTRODUCTION

Most needlepointers get cold feet when they have completed stitching and are confronted with blocking and mounting their work into finished articles. There is a good reason for this! A lot of time and effort has gone into the canvas embroidery, and no one wants to assume the responsibility for ruining the piece by cutting an edge off at the wrong moment or putting the lining on inside out. In addition, many people do not have sewing machines and other equipment that is needed to put the projects together.

Before saying "No!" to yourself again, remember that you can save a substantial amount of money by doing the work yourself, and you will have the satisfaction of having made a decorative art object from start to finish. Read the notes and instructions in Chapter 5 for the piece you are working on to see if you have at your disposal the equipment and materials needed to mount the project. If so, why not give it a try?

## IS YOUR PIECE READY FOR BLOCKING?

No doubt you have discovered by now that it is much easier to correct errors in your work as they occur than to leave them until the end when they may be forgotten. Before preparing your piece for blocking, check again to see that all errors have been corrected and that there are no missing stitches. This is your last chance!

**Make sure there are no missing stitches and that all errors have been corrected before blocking your work. Striped sampler by Carol Rome.**

Hold the piece up to a strong light and notice if canvas shows through anywhere. You may have left out a compensating stitch, or you may have had to end a strand a few stitches before the end of a row. Fuzzy ends sticking through the surface of the work should be pulled to the back or trimmed off.

Have you added the decorative overstitching that you planned to incorporate into the design? What about a monogram? Check the piece for dirt, removing any smudges or stains now.

The last thing to do before blocking is to make sure the canvas edges are still securely hemmed or taped. This part of the canvas will be under a lot of tension in the blocking process. Repeat the taping or hemming job if it looks weak.

## BLOCKING

Blocking is the most important factor in the finished appearance of a needlepoint piece. A piece mounted with beautiful fabric and cording will still look amateurish if it is lumpy and crooked.

Some pieces probably won't require a heavy blocking job. However, some of the original crispness of every piece has been lost in the working sessions, and all pieces should be restiffened before mounting. Other pieces may

Mrs. Edward Oppenheimer of Ames, Iowa, has done a good job blocking this piece. Note the squared corners and even, straight diagonal lines.

appear to be absolutely hopeless cases, and you will wonder how any amount of blocking could restore them to their intended shape.

Almost all crookedness, rolling and lumps can be eliminated by good blocking, provided that you have avoided using Continental stitch and have worked with a normal tension. In very extreme, "incurable" cases, some of the needlepoint may have to be sacrificed in the mounting process to make the finished piece square. Generally, the more stretching that is needed, the more water you will have to use to block the piece straight.

The first time you do a fairly wet blocking job, do not think you have ruined your chef d'oeuvre when you discover that the stiff needlepointed piece has been transformed into a soggy, slimy mess. This is perfectly normal! Proceed, following the instructions. After the piece is dry, it will be as good as new.

1. Choose a blocking board. Some people prefer a wood board, and others prefer a section of insulation board, which is a compressed material slightly porous and softer than a wood board. The board should be at least a few inches larger all around than the piece being blocked. A piece of board 2' x 4' is a size that will accommodate a variety of projects. Cover the board with muslin or clean paper and mark on the covering the original dimensions of the needlepoint and the center vertical and horizontal lines. Use an *indelible* laundry marking pen.

2. Press the needlepoint piece on both sides with a very damp cloth or towel placed between the iron and the work. This usually provides sufficient moisture for blocking a piece. Extremely crooked pieces may have to be totally immersed in water at this point. The excess can be forced out by placing the piece between clean towels and exerting pressure with your hands. Do not wring.

3. Slash the selvage at 2" or 3" intervals. The selvage is much more closely woven than the rest of the canvas and tends to be shorter along the side. If left intact, the selvage may prevent you from pulling the piece square. Do *not* cut off the taped or hemmed edges.

A damp towel is placed between the iron and the wrong side of the piece to be blocked.

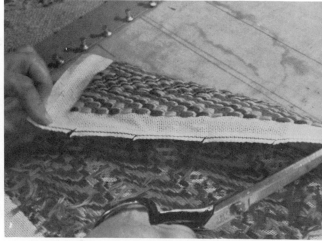

Slash the selvage at regular intervals.

4. Place the piece face down on the board matching the center lines of the piece with the vertical and horizontal lines marked on the board covering. (If there is a great deal of raised work, the piece will have to be blocked face up.) Use rustproof tacks, brass or aluminum nails or pushpins to hold the piece in place. Staples are not preferred since they tend to pierce and cut the mesh.

Tack 1 side down at 1″ intervals from one end to the other. Next tack a side perpendicular to the first side. Check to see if you have a true right angle at the corner and if the dimensions of the canvas match those you marked on the board covering. Tack the other 2 sides, pulling as much as is necessary to get square corners and straight sides.

5. Spray the back of the piece with a liberal amount of a good sizing while it is still damp and tacked to the board.

Pull tight and make sure the taped or hemmed canvas edges are securely pinned down at 1-inch intervals.

Check all four corners with a drafter's square. Note how the selvage edge has spread out.

6. Let the piece dry thoroughly. This may take overnight or longer if the piece is large and heavy.

7. Remove the piece from the board. You will notice that the original stiffness of the piece has been restored. Trim the excess blank margin to the specifications of your project only *after* you are certain that the needle-point is perfectly square. If it is not square, repeat the blocking process.

8. If the stitches seem to be somewhat flat, hold a steam iron just above the work or press the piece gently with a damp cloth and moderate iron and fluff up the wool.

It should be mentioned that there exists a great deal of controversy over what is a proper blocking job and what isn't. You may encounter people who tack the work and then moisten it. Others tack the sides in a different order. Some don't slash the selvage. And some do not even believe in using moisture at all in the blocking process.

The method of blocking described here has been developed over many years of professional experience, and it has been used successfully on literally thousands of pieces. While you may innovate a few personal touches in the blocking process, you will want to follow the essential procedures in the order given for best results.

## MOUNTING TERMINOLOGY

The following is a list of miscellaneous hints and definitions that should help you get started on blocking and mounting your own work.

*Basting:* Making long in and out running stitches with heavy-duty thread to hold one piece to another and to prevent slipping.

*Binding Stitch:* A whipping stitch made with yarn to join edges of canvas together. (See page 218 for details.)

*Blindstitch:* This is a method of sewing one piece to another with thread so that the stitches don't show from the right side.

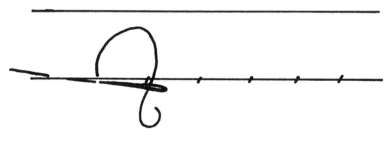

Working on a blindstitch.

*Clipping Curves:* Cording, needlepoint and backing seam allowances should be clipped or cut with the points of your scissors to make the seam lie open and flat when it is pressed. Be careful not to cut into the seam line stitching or a small hole will show through on the right side of the project.

*Gluing:* Several of the projects in this book call for gluing in the mounting process. It is recommended that you use thin, evenly spread coatings of Elmer's or Sobo for best results. To aid in the drying process, place the glued items between heavy books.

*Grain of the Canvas:* The lengthwise and crosswise directions of the mesh make up the grain of the canvas. The canvas is on true grain when the lengthwise and crosswise mesh intersect at right angles. Occasionally, it may be necessary to pull the canvas from 2 opposite corners to get it on true grain.

*Hammering:* Some very bulky edges and corners may have to be hammered to get them to lie flat. Place a clean cloth between the needlepoint and hammer.

*Machine-stitching:* Many of the projects in this book require the use of a sewing machine for mounting. Make sure you use a heavy-duty needle in the machine. You may want to pin and/or baste the project pieces in place to avoid shifting while you are machine stitching. Be sure that you use a heavy-duty thread that matches the color of the project backing or lining. Mercerized cotton thread is a good choice for most purposes.

The most important thing to remember is that you will have to sew into the needlepoint work a little when seaming the project pieces. This means that you should have a few extra rows of needlepoint all around the edge of your piece than can be sacrificed during the mounting process. The greatest loss is at the corners of pillows. Here, for instance, 3 rows of Diagonal Tent on 14 count canvas may have to be incorporated into the seam to keep the pillow from having a dog-eared shape.

*Miter:* The term mitering appears in many of the project write-ups. In this process you will cut off the canvas at the corners at an angle to within 2 or 3 mesh of the worked area. The remaining excess is folded down at the corner, and the sides are folded down on top of this to make nice clean edges with a minimum of bulk. Another method of mitering is to cut a square of excess canvas from the corners, folding under the remainder.

Mitering the corners, Method I, to eliminate bulk.

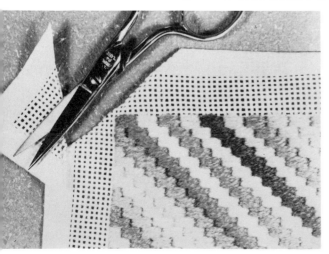

Mitering the corners, Method II.

*Pressing:* You will want your iron handy when blocking and mounting a needlepoint piece. The most important thing to remember about pressing is that the iron should *never* come in direct contact with the right side of the needlepoint stitching. If this happens, the stitches get mashed down and look unattractively shiny like a suit that has been cleaned too many times. Use a steam iron to press open seams. Pat the work with the iron rather than rubbing the iron back and forth. Place a clean damp cloth or towel between the right side of the work and the iron if you need to press the whole piece flat.

*Press-on Pellon:* This is a synthetic, spun fabric backing which adheres to another surface when ironed down. It is excellent to use as an interlining to give extra body to a piece and to prevent it from crawling out of shape. The back of the needlepoint should be free of uncut tails and messy ends to get a good bond between the Pellon and the needlepoint.

*Seam Allowance:* Seam allowance is that amount of needlepoint and/or fabric that is needed to make a strong seam. If too narrow a seam allowance is used, the seam is apt to pull apart. Too large a seam allowance means that fabric or stitching is being wasted. Some projects have special seam allowance requirements. However, ½″ is usually sufficient for a strong, durable seam. Remember that part of this seam will be needlepoint stitching. Be sure to make enough extra rows to keep your border from being eaten away in the mounting process.

*Slashing:* Slashing the selvage during blocking means to make long clips or cuts into the selvage at regular intervals. This allows the selvage to spread out.

*Tacking:* Tacking is to hand-sew 2 pieces together with tiny stitches to hold them secure.

*Tapering the Corners:* Part of the right angle of the blank canvas margin and backing fabric corners should be cut away to a taper to prevent the finished pillow or pincushion from having a dog-eared look. This trimming is done before the pieces are assembled.

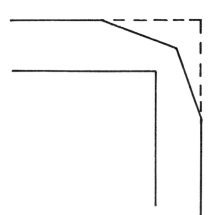

Tapering a corner. Use the tapered edges as a guide when sewing the seams.

*Trimming the Excess:* No excess canvas should be cut from the needle-point piece until blocking has been done. Then the excess can be trimmed with sharp scissors to within ½″ of the worked area, except when the project specifications call for different measurements. Use the tapered edges as a guide when stitching.

*Velcro:* Velcro is an ingenious fastening or closure made of 2 strips of man-made "burs" that stick to each other tenaciously when they come in contact. To open, simply pull the strips apart. These strips can be glued or sewn to the backing surface and to the wrong side of the needlepoint work.

*Whipstitch:* This is an over and under stitch sewn by hand to join 2 pieces together. Regular heavy-duty thread is used. The stitch can be seen from the right side of the work, making it less versatile than the blindstitch.

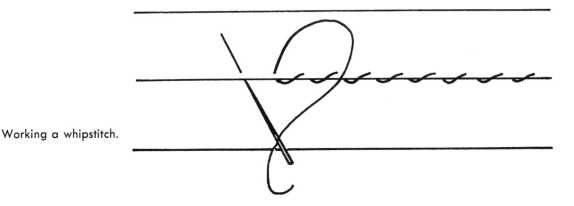

Working a whipstitch.

## CORDING

Cording gives many projects a professional finish, and surprisingly, it is not difficult to make. You can choose between cording that is made of yarn that matches your needlepoint and cording covered with fabric that matches the project backing.

*Braided Yarn Cord:* Simple braid can be used as a border or for special effects such as "real pigtails," picture hangers and closures. Take 3 or 4 groups of yarn strands in one or more colors that compliment your project and braid them together, tying them off at each end. Whip the braided cording down over a finished seam on the outside of the piece.

*Fabric-covered Cord:* Fabric-covered cord is the most popular kind used to finish the seams of a project.

1. Choose the appropriate gauge cording for your project at a notions store. A small object should have fine cord, a larger object can have thicker cord.

2. Cut the cord the length you need to surround the project plus 2″ seam allowance. Double the amount if 2 sides are to be corded.

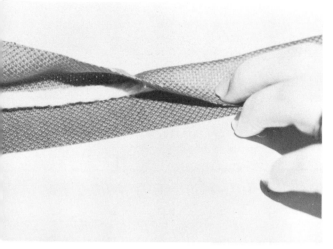

Cut strips of fabric to cover cording.

Use the zipper foot as a guide when stitching the cording.

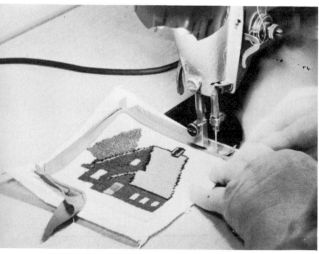

When applying the cording to your finished piece, clip the corners for ease.

3. The fabric covering for the cord can be cut from the backing fabric. The 1½″ to 2″ wide strips should be cut on the bias for cording rounded edges and from selvage to selvage (widthwise) for straight edges. The distance around the edges to be corded plus 2″ gives you the proper length.

4. Fold the fabric strip over the cord. Machine-baste close to the cord using the zipper foot as a guide.

5. Lay the covered cord on the right side of the needlepoint piece along the seamline. The raw edge of the cord will face outward to match the raw edges of the project. Pin and baste the cording in place. Clip the raw cording edges almost to the stitching at the corners and around any curves. Overlap the cording as inconspicuously as possible where the 2 ends meet.

If you have corded the edge of an insert that needs no backing, all you need to do is turn the raw cording edges to the back and tack them down. Proceed with the mounting instructions for that project.

When working on a project that will need backing, the cording should be placed between the right side of the needlepoint and the right side of the backing along the seamline. You will sew through all thicknesses along the seamline and then turn the piece right side out.

## FRINGE

Fringe gives a festive look to a finished piece of needlepoint. It is used instead of cording. Ready-made fringe can be used or you can make your own with strands of yarn that match your project.

1. Loop several strands of yarn back and forth like ribbon candy, making the loops 1″ more than double the length you want the fringe to be.

2. Machine-stitch 2 rows about 1″ apart along the center of the row of loops.

3. Cut between the 2 rows of stitching, and you will have 2 lengths of fringe ready to go. All that is needed is to clip the loops and trim them even.

Fringe is applied to the finished piece according to the instructions for cording. The raw ends face out toward the edges of the piece on the right side. The fringe is basted in place along the seamline, and then the piece is mounted as usual.

A row of fringe *can* be made right on a finished piece such as at the ends of a rug. Needlepoint the design up to the last row before the boundary. Fold the canvas edge under so that 2 mesh are on the fold.

1. Work a row of Turkey Tufting through both layers to make the fringe. Clipping the loops after the row is complete is optional.

2. Or cut strands of yarn twice as long as the desired fringe length and fold each strand in half. Using a crochet hook, pull the loop from the back to the front of the canvas using the first free hole. Pull the 2 strands through the loop and pull tight. Repeat in each adjoining hole until the row of holes is filled.

Making fringe.

## TASSELS

Tassels look best when they are made of yarn that matches that used in your project. They are used with cording or fringe or alone.

    1. Put together several lengths of yarn (the more strands the fuller the tassel), cutting them just over twice the length you want the finished tassel to be.

    2. Tie the group in the middle with a piece of yarn and make several knots to give it extra strength.

3. Fold the lengths of yarn in half and wrap another length of yarn round and round the tassle about ½″ from the top. Tie this on one side and then the other and smooth the remaining tails down into the bulk of the tassel.

4. Trim the bottom and fluff the tassel out.

Use the knotted length of yarn to attach the tassel in place at the project seamline.

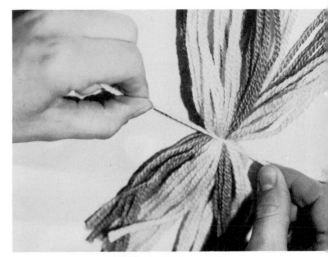

Making a tassel.

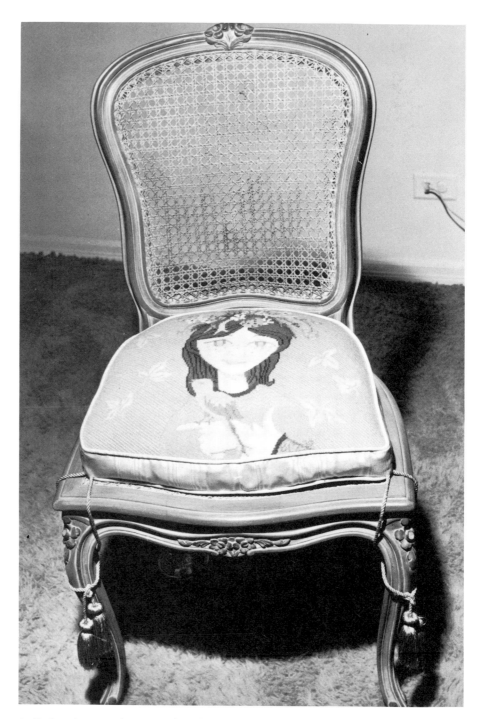

Girl's head on a chair seat by Mrs. Harry Powell Wilson, Jr., Denver. Note the elegant backing and cords and tassels.

## BACKING AND LINING

The fabric you use to back a needlepoint pillow or to line a variety of projects can make or break the finished appearance of the work. There is an endless selection of fabrics from which to choose. Your choice should match or compliment the colors and formality of the needlepoint piece. If you have used soft colors, a bold, bright-colored backing or lining will "kill" your design. If the colors of your design are bright, the use of a quiet color in the backing or lining fabric will make the finished piece appear dull.

The fabric you choose should be durable and relatively stain resistant. Remember that the right choice can add years to the life of your needlepoint piece. Do not choose a lining that will add bulk to the piece; this is especially true of smaller projects.

Velvet is one of the most popular backings for pillows. It is very attractive when worked up. However, be forewarned that velvet has a tendency to creep and crawl under the needle, making it somewhat difficult to handle. Velvet would not be suitable for lining a project because of the bulk it would add to the piece.

Moiré silk is excellent for use on all small projects and many of the larger ones. It is relatively thin and slippery and looks elegant when it is made up into finished pieces.

Other frequently used backing and lining fabrics are sailcloth (totebags, director's chairs and tennis racquet covers), linen and fine cotton (pillows and book jackets), and burlap. Some of these fabrics are available already treated with Scotch-garding.

Generally, backing and lining fabric pieces are cut to the dimensions of the canvas after it has been blocked and trimmed. Remember to buy enough fabric to make boxings and cording if these are to be included in the finishing process.

## JOINING CANVAS

Learning the methods for joining canvas can save you a great deal of trouble and expense. This is a skill you will use frequently, especially if you mount your own work. Opposite edges of a needlepointed piece must be joined together in the mounting process. Also, there are times when it is necessary to join 2 or more separate pieces of canvas together. Often rugs have to be worked in sections since the whole piece would be too cumbersome to handle. You may change your mind about how you want to use a finished piece and find that you are going to have to enlarge it for the new destination.

Whichever of the following methods of seaming you choose to work with, keep in mind these hints. It is much easier to join 2 unworked canvas areas together than 2 worked areas. If you are planning a project with 2 or more pieces, leave several rows unworked where the pieces will be joined. The canvas sections you join should be the same gauge and dimensions, and each piece should be worked with the same "up" direction (selvages should be at the sides). The pieces should be blocked separately and must be perfectly square before seaming.

### Method I: Overlapped Needlepoint

1. Place the 2 pieces of canvas together so that ½″ of the unworked margins adjacent to the needlepoint are overlapping. Baste this double thickness together with carpet thread, being careful that each mesh is perfectly lined up and that all areas of the design match. Do not cut off the taped or hemmed edges yet even though they may seem to be in the way.

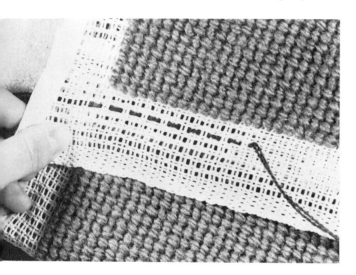

Baste the two pieces of canvas together, carefully matching mesh and design.

2. Work 2 or 3 rows of needlepoint down the center of the overlapped layers to secure the double thickness. Then cut off the excess margins and needlepoint as many rows as are needed to fill in the unworked area. There will be no apparent added bulk, and the resulting seam is very strong and durable.

Needlepoint a couple of rows to secure the two pieces before trimming the excess.

Trim the excess and fill in the remaining un-worked rows.

3. If any cut mesh ends poke through to the surface, work them to the back of the canvas with your needle. This method is excellent for piecing together several sections of a large project such as a rug.

Make sure any cut mesh ends are poked through to the back of the canvas.

*Method II: Machine-stitching and Needlepoint*

1. Lay together 2 pieces that are worked to within 1 or 2 rows of the design boundary right sides together. Match mesh and design up carefully and baste the 2 pieces together. Machine-stitch down the seamline. Open out the seam allowance and press the seam open and flat. Cut off the excess taped or hemmed canvas edges.

Baste and machine stitch a seam, carefully matching mesh and design.

Needlepoint the empty rows, joining the two pieces. Do not stitch through the seam allowance at the back of the canvas.

2. Needlepoint the few remaining unworked rows of design as though the canvas were one continuous piece. Avoid stitching through the seam allowance on the wrong side of the canvas.

3. Tack the open seam allowance loosely in place.

The advantage of using this method is the absence of any extra bulk at the seam. The machine-stitching is strong; however, you will not have the added strength of overlapped needlepoint stitching. This method is suitable for seaming rug projects.

### Method III: Machine-seaming

Machine-seaming is used to join together opposite edges of a piece during the mounting process. You will need to use a heavy-duty needle in your machine when working with needlepoint, which is quite bulky.

Stitch along the seamline from the wrong side of the needlepoint according to the specifications of your project. It is not recommended that you use this method of seaming to join rug sections, as it is difficult to sew a perfectly straight line, and an uneven seam would detract from the smooth surface of the finished piece.

### Method IV: The Binding Stitch

The binding stitch method may be the most versatile, inexpensive way to seam canvas together. It can be used to join separate pieces of canvas *and* opposite edges of the same piece. In addition, it is used for finishing raw edges. As you can see, the binding stitch is an important stitch to include in your repertoire.

The stitch is merely a whipping stitch that crosses back and forth over the outer edge(s) of folded canvas, creating an attractive "V" pattern. It is very strong and durable.

1 double strand = 2½" running
1 color
(1-1-1)-2-3
do not rotate

To finish a single edge, fold the edge of the canvas just above a worked section so that 2 mesh are on top. To join 2 separate pieces, fold the edges of the canvas so that 1 mesh from each piece is on top.

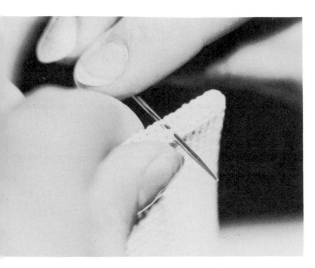

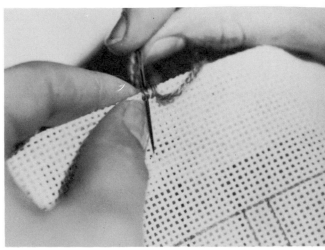

Make sure 2 mesh are at the fold when starting the binding stitch.

Starting the binding stitch.

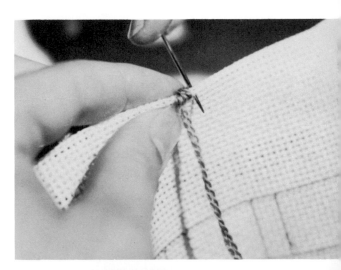

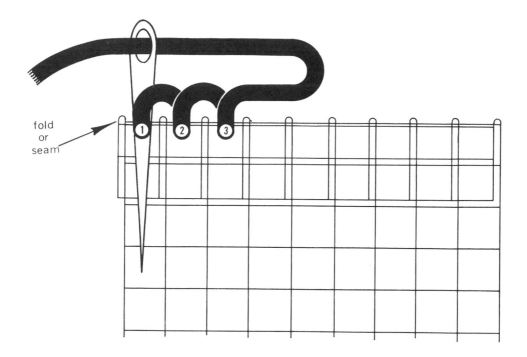

fold
or
seam

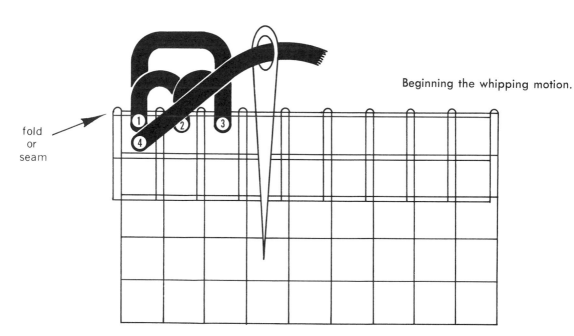

fold
or
seam

Beginning the whipping motion.

A "bird's-eye view" of the binding stitch.

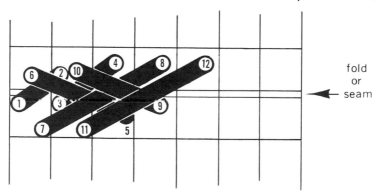

fold
or
seam

Working from left to right, with the right side of the needlepoint toward you, come from the back to the front 3 times. Then backtrack 2 mesh and come straight through from back to front, reusing the first hole. The next stitch moves ahead 3 mesh to the right to the next free hole. From this point on, after each forward progression of 3 mesh, you will backtrack 2 mesh in a whipping motion.

Be sure to match mesh to mesh when turning a corner or joining 2 pieces of canvas together so the sides will come out evenly. You may have to stitch over the corners a second time for adequate coverage. Miter the corners from the wrong side and clip out excess canvas. Turn down and tack in place trimmed edges where necessary to eliminate unnecessary bulk.

When joining 2 sides of the same piece, work from the outer edges to the fold. When you come back to the starting point, overlap a few stitches of the bound area so no canvas will show through and for added strength.

*Note:* When working with the binding stitch, it is sometimes easier to wait until all edges are bound before trimming excess canvas to prevent possible raveling.

## CANVAS APPLIQUÉS

A worked section of canvas can be appliquéd to an unworked section of the same or another gauge canvas. Historically, this technique was used to work an area of extremely fine detail stitched on gauze into the main design. Sometimes the inserted appliqué was padded to give realism and depth to the piece; this was called stump work.

First make the appliqué insert, allowing the usual 1½″ blank margins on all sides. The canvas edges should be taped or hemmed. Work the piece, then block it before it is appliquéd to the second piece of canvas. Do not work on the base piece, the area that the insert will cover.

1. Trim the excess margin of the insert to ¼″. Turn the edges under, mitering the corners, clipping curves and pressing flat. Tack the margin in place to the wrong side of the insert. The edges can be machine-stitched for added strength.

2. Place the insert over the unworked area of the base piece of canvas. Blindstitch the insert in place. If there are any unfinished rows on the base piece, fill them in. An Outline stitch, cording or braid can be used around the perimeter of the appliquéd insert to cover any rough edges.

## SCOTCH-GARD

After your project has been blocked and mounted, spray it with Scotch-gard, following the directions on the can for upholstery fabric. This treatment gives added protection to the work from spills and soiling.

# Further Reading

## Design:

Dover Books on Art and the Dover Pictorial Archives Series. Dover Publications, Inc., New York. (Paperback books with hundreds of line drawings of designs from many sources and countries.)

Placek, Karl J. *Ornaments and Designs.* New York: Bonanza Books, 1951.

Rhodes, Mary. *Ideas for Canvas Work.* 28 Union Street, Newton Centre, Mass. 02159: Charles T. Branford Company, 1970.

## Ecclesiastical Work:

Dean, Beryl. *Ecclesiastical Embroidery.* Newton Centre, Mass.: Charles T. Branford Company, 1961.

## General Reference:

*Craft Shops/Galleries U.S.A.,* 1970. American Crafts Council, 29 West 53rd Street, New York 10019.

*Embroidery.* The quarterly publication of The Embroiderers' Guild, 73 Wimpole Street, London, WIM 8AX, England.

*Needle Arts.* The quarterly publication of The Embroiderers' Guild of America, Inc., 120 East 56th Street, New York 10022.

## History:

Freeman, Margaret B. *The St. Martin Embroideries.* New York: The Metropolitan Museum of Art, 1968.

Harbeson, Georgiana Brown. *American Needlework.* New York: Bonanza Books, 1968.

Huish, Marcus. *Samplers and Tapestry Embroideries.* New York: Dover Publications, 1970.

Symonds, Mary, and Preece, Louisa. *Needlework through the Ages.* Pts. I & II. London: Hodder & Stoughton, Ltd., 1928.

## Lettering:

Hunt, W. Ben., and Hunt, Ed. C. *101 Alphabets.* Milwaukee: The Bruce Publishing Company, 1958.

Nesbitt, Alexander, ed. *A Handbook of Decorative Alphabets and Initials.* New York: Dover Publications, 1959.

Russell, Pat. *Lettering for Embroidery.* New York: Van Nostrand Reinhold, 1971.

Turbayne, A. A. *Monograms and Ciphers.* New York: Dover Publications, 1968.

# Resources

The Embroiderers' Guild of America, Inc., New York City.

The Bayou Bend Collection of the Museum of Fine Arts, Houston, Texas. Mr. David Warren, Director.

Colonial Williamsburg Foundation, Williamsburg, Virginia. Miss Mildred B. Lanier, Curator of Textiles, and Miss Sandra C. Schaffer.

The Metropolitan Museum of Art, New York City. Miss Jean Mailey, Associate Curator, Textile Study Room.

Historic Deerfield, Inc., Deerfield, Massachusetts. Mr. Peter Spang III, Curator, and Mrs. John Banta.

Cooper-Hewitt Museum of Decorative Arts and Design, New York City. Miss Alice Beer, Consultant.

# Index

Main stitch names are printed in SMALL CAPITALS, alternate stitch names are in *italics;* s indicates the stitch number, and p indicates the project number.